AF872677

The Sacred Witness

Trauma-Informed Care for Holistic Healers, Coaches, and Facilitators

Auroara Leigh, MEd

Wellness Anthropologist | Educator | Founder, The Healership Academy

You chose this work because something in you knew the world needed more people willing to truly witness another human being.

The Healership Academy | www.simplysacred.ca

Copyright © 2026 Simply Sacred Solutions

All rights reserved. No part of this publication may be reproduced, distributed, or transmitted in any form or by any means without the prior written permission of the publisher, except for brief quotations in reviews.

Published by Simply Sacred Solutions
www.simplysacred.ca

ISBN: 978-1-7781082-1-1

Printed in Canada

First Edition

Contents

• • •

• • •

FORWARD

There are moments in one's professional walk, where you encounter someone whose work is born not only from intellect, but from deep inquiry, lived experience, and an authentic desire to help others in a deep and meaningful way. Meeting Auroara Leigh was one of those moments for me.

As a therapist, I have spent years witnessing the profound impact trauma can have on the nervous system, relationships, identity, and a person's sense of safety in the world. I have also witnessed how many individuals are turning not only toward licensed mental health professionals, but toward coaches, spiritual practitioners, energy healers, mentors, and wellness guides in search of meaning, connection, transformation, and healing.

This shift reflects a collective longing for approaches that honour both psychological insight and the deeper human need for purpose, spirituality, embodiment, and belonging. Yet, with that shift comes an important responsibility. When people enter healing spaces carrying trauma, vulnerability, grief, or dysregulation, good intentions alone are not enough. Without trauma-informed understanding, even well-meaning guidance can unintentionally reinforce shame, dependency, overwhelm, or emotional harm. This is why the work you are about to read matters.

Auroara brings a rare combination of intellectual rigor, relational depth, and compassionate curiosity to this conversation. Her background in education and psychological anthropology gives her a nuanced understanding of human behaviour, diversity, meaning-making, and relational systems. What stands out even more, is the care with which she approaches the ethical dimensions of healing work.

This book invites readers into a more grounded and responsible way of supporting human transformation. A way that is rooted in self-awareness, attunement, humility, nervous system awareness, and respect for the complexity of trauma.

This work acknowledges the value that can exist within spiritual and alternative healing spaces while also emphasizing the importance of discernment, scope, accountability, and ongoing learning. In a time when healing language has become trendy and the phrase "trauma-informed" a common buzz word, this perspective is both refreshing and necessary.

Trauma-informed practice asks us to move in a way that we can understand clients' protection, survival, and resilience. It calls practitioners to become more aware not only of others' wounds, but of their own influence, limitations, and responsibility within the healing relationship.

The invitation within these pages is not toward perfection, but toward consciousness. Toward deeper integrity. Toward creating spaces where people feel safer, more empowered, and more fully seen in their humanity.

I believe this book will serve as an important resource for coaches, spiritual practitioners, and healing professionals who genuinely wish to support others with greater wisdom, compassion, and care. May it contribute meaningfully to a healing culture that is both heart-centered and responsibly informed.

— Ashlea Lawrenson RTC, BA
Heart Centered EMDR
www.heart-centered.ca

A Note Before You Begin

Trauma-informed care is a way of being. It is a natural orientation toward the humans in front of you, rooted in the understanding that every person carries experience in their body and that this experience shapes how they move through the world.

This book is written for anyone who holds space for others: teachers, facilitators, yoga instructors, life coaches, practitioners, acupuncturists, bodyworkers, dentists, leaders of women's and men's circles, spiritual guides, community organizers, and anyone whose work places them in relationship with another person's vulnerability.

This is an educational resource. It is grounded in trauma-informed pedagogy, somatic awareness, and the lived experience of working with people across many contexts. It does not represent or replace licensed clinical care, medical treatment, psychiatric intervention, or psychological therapy. Nothing in this book constitutes a diagnosis, prescription, or clinical recommendation.

Reading this book does not eliminate the possibility of harm, bias, or rupture within your practice. It does not certify you as a trauma-informed practitioner. It does not guarantee the safety of any session, ceremony, or interaction. The work of holding space is living work, and it requires ongoing learning, self-reflection, supervision, and humility.

If someone in your care is in crisis or presenting with symptoms beyond your scope, refer them to a qualified professional.

The author and publisher assume no liability for actions taken based on the contents of this book. You are responsible for your own practice, your own discernment, and the wellbeing of the people you serve.

This work is offered with deep respect for the many traditions, lineages, and ways of knowing that have held humanity through suffering for millennia. May it serve you well.

I did not write this book because I have all the answers. I wrote it because I have sat in enough circles, facilitated enough rooms, and held enough hands to know that the people doing this work, the coaches, the healers, the facilitators, the workshop leaders, the community guides, often have enormous hearts and not nearly enough tools.

I know this because I was one of them.

Years before I held a Master of Education from UBC, before I specialized in trauma informed safe spaces for group environments, or had built a methodology, before I had named words like trau-mour and **healership**, I was a healer without a **container**. I was a guide without a map. I was pouring myself into spaces with people who needed far more than good intentions, and I was learning, sometimes at great cost to them and to me, what it meant to be truly trauma-informed.

The work I do now, through Simply Sacred Solutions and through years of developing culturally safe, trauma-informed education across healthcare, education and community sectors, has taught me something I want every healer to know: the quality of your presence is not determined by your training alone. It is shaped by your willingness to keep learning, keep refining, keep asking what does this person actually need from me right now, and am I the one who can provide it?

This book exists because trauma is not rare. It is woven through the fabric of human experience across every culture, every generation, every socioeconomic reality. And the people seeking holistic support from you have often tried other doors and found them locked. They come to you carrying what has never been witnessed. What has never been named. What has never been honoured. You are the door they are trying now. This book is your preparation.

I wrote this with you held in my heart the entire time. Every healer reading this chose this path for a reason. Let this book be part of what makes your reason sacred.

With love and deep respect for your journey, **Auroara Leigh, MEd**

Wellness Anthropologist | Founder, The Healership Academy

Who This Book Is For

If you have ever picked up the phone at two in the morning, this book was written for you.

It is also written for everyone else who keeps ending up in the room where another human is falling apart. The sister. The husband. The best friend. The auntie whose porch is always open. The son sitting across from the mother whose voice has started to shake. The elder who has been holding ceremony for a community that has never stopped grieving. The teacher whose classroom became a shelter on a Tuesday morning. The nurse. The social worker. The addictions counsellor. The kitchen-table therapist who has no letters after her name.

You were probably called to this work long before anyone gave it a name. The capacity lived in you before the title did. If you later earned a degree, the degree refined what was already there. It did not create it.

Others of you never sought a credential. You became the one people come to anyway. The manager pulled into conversations your job description does not name. The youth worker who hears what policy documents pretend does not happen. The elder asked to speak the old words to someone who has forgotten what land felt like under bare feet. The community leader. The chaplain. The doula. The executive assistant who has become, without anyone calling it that, the emotional infrastructure of the office.

This is the circle this book is written for.

The Circle Is Widening Because It Has To

For a long time, the teaching of how to hold another human being in their hardest moment was locked behind clinical training, behind certifications, behind degrees. That gate has not served us. The old container, the one that asked us to outsource all our grief and terror to licensed professionals, was always going to crack. It is cracking now.

What is rising through the cracks is older than any credential. The ancient practice of one human staying with another. One body calming another body. One voice meeting another voice in the dark. This book is an attempt to honour that practice and to offer some tools for it. The work has always belonged to us. The circle was never supposed to be small.

If you are a trained practitioner, you belong here too. You were a friend, a sister, a son, or a coworker before you were a practitioner. The everyday witness lives inside you still. Returning to that root tends to deepen the professional work.

Who Is Welcome Here

For the woman who was told she is too sensitive and is starting to understand her sensitivity as a skill.

For the man who grew up being told to stop crying and who is learning to sit with someone else's tears without flinching, and who sometimes surprises himself by crying too.

For the person whose first language is not English, whose way of carrying grief is not named in the Western trauma canon, who needed a book that did not demand assimilation as the price of entry.

For the Indigenous woman holding the intergenerational weight of what settler colonialism did to her family, and who is finding her way back to the medicine the land has always known.

For the neurodivergent reader whose nervous system does not follow the textbook maps. For the queer and trans reader whose sense of safety has always been a negotiation. For the disabled reader who has been told, one too many times, that trauma healing happens on somebody else's timeline. The pages ahead try to make room.

For the person who is doing the work on themselves at the same time they are holding it for others. That is most of us. You are not a fraud for being in both places at once. Human is the qualification.

For the body workers. The yoga teachers whose students sometimes shake in shavasana and do not know why. The breathwork facilitators who hold rooms that become shaking rooms. The acupuncturists whose clients start weeping when the needle goes in. The chiropractors whose adjustments release more than tension. The massage therapists, the craniosacral practitioners, the Reiki practitioners, the somatic movement teachers. Bodies carry story, and when a body receives skilled care, the story rises. Trauma-informed witnessing is part of your work whether anyone trained you for it or not.

For the teachers and educators. The classroom teacher whose Tuesday morning becomes a disclosure. The professor whose student emails at two in the morning. The workshop facilitator who sees a face change during a group exercise. The continuing education instructor whose curriculum touches something a participant was not ready to meet. If you teach in rooms where humans are learning, you are holding nervous systems. That is part of the role.

Trauma-informed practice is a basic literacy for being in a room with another human. This book is for everyone willing to grow in that literacy.

What This Book Does Not Ask of You

This book does not ask you to become a therapist. It does not ask you to diagnose, interpret, or treat. It does not ask you to carry what is not yours to carry. It does not ask you to hold what another human is only willing to metabolize with a professional.

This book asks one thing. That you be willing to stay. Willing to breathe. Willing to let another human feel what they feel without needing to rescue, fix, perform, or flee. That willingness is the whole practice. The chapters ahead offer shape for it.

An Invitation

If any of these readers sound like you, even a little, welcome. The circle has been waiting for you. The work has been waiting for you. Your presence is part of what changes the story for someone else, and for the generations after them.

Turn the page when you are ready.

PART ONE

Foundations

• • •

Before we step into the room with anyone else, we have to know what we are carrying, what we are meeting, and what the word trauma actually means once we put down the versions we inherited.

These first chapters give you the ground. What trauma is. Who you already are as a witness, whether or not that word has been used about you before. How the nervous system works underneath every other conversation this book will have.

Sit here a while. Let the language land. This is the ground that holds the whole book, and the ground underneath your own feet when you sit across from someone who is unraveling.

CHAPTER ONE

What Trauma Actually Is

Before we can care for someone in their pain, we need to understand what that pain is and what it is not.

The word trauma is everywhere now. It lives in social media captions and wellness retreats, in therapy circles and casual conversation. And while the growing awareness is meaningful, the proliferation has also created a fog. People are using the word to describe everything from a difficult childhood to a bad day at work, and in that fog, healers sometimes lose the precision they need.

Trauma Is a Response, Not a Diagnosis

Trauma is not what happened to someone. Trauma is what happened inside someone as a result of an overwhelming experience that exceeded their capacity to cope in that moment.

This is essential. You are not working with damaged people. You are working with people who had completely normal nervous system responses to abnormal circumstances. Their bodies did exactly what bodies are designed to do: they adapted. They protected. They survived.

An anti-**pathologizing** lens means you hold this understanding in the room with you at all times. The person across from you is responding. They have always been responding. Their responses make sense. They always did.

The Four Primary Stress Response States

Fight

The body mobilizes for conflict. You may see jaw tension, a raised voice, defensiveness, argumentativeness, or apparent aggression. The person may push back against your facilitation because their nervous system is trying to create safety through force. What presents as resistance is a body reaching for protection.

Flight

The body mobilizes for escape. You may see fidgeting, avoidance of eye contact, distraction, checking phones, an urgency to leave or redirect the conversation. The person's system is trying to create safety through distance.

Freeze

The body shuts down mobilization entirely. You may see a flat affect, **dissociation**, silence, a dazed or checked out quality. The person may appear calm but be entirely unreachable. This is the nervous system playing dead because neither fight nor flight felt safe.

Fawn

The body attempts to create safety through appeasement. You may see excessive agreeableness, over-compliance, smiling through pain, telling you what they think you want to hear. This is one of the most important responses for facilitators to understand because it can look like everything is going well when it is not.

What Trauma Looks Like in the Body

Trauma lives in the nervous system, not just the mind. The body holds the **traum-our**, as the research consistently shows, which means the healing must also reach the body. Understanding the primary nervous system states will change how you see every client interaction.

The Fawn Response: A Facilitator's Crucial Knowledge

Of all four stress responses, fawn is the one most likely to go undetected in a facilitation or coaching space, and it is one of the most important to understand.

Fawning is the practice of managing perceived danger through pleasing, agreeing, and suppressing one's authentic response in order to keep the peace and maintain a sense of safety in relationship. It is often developed in childhoods where conflict or authenticity was unsafe. Where the cost of saying no was too high.

In your space, this means the person across from you may be smiling and nodding while internally flooded. They may say the exercise was helpful when it was overwhelming. They may agree to explore a topic they are not ready for simply because they do not know they have the right to decline.

You may never know. And that is exactly why this book exists.

Intergenerational Trauma and Generational Healing

Trauma does not begin and end with a single lifetime. The science of **epigenetics** and the wisdom of Indigenous and ancestral knowledge traditions both confirm what many healing practitioners have always felt to be true: pain is passed down through bloodlines, through survival strategies, through learned beliefs about the world and what is safe within it.

When you sit with someone, you are often sitting with generations. The grief that surfaces in a workshop circle may have roots that predate the person in front of you by decades or centuries. This is especially true for Indigenous peoples, for descendants of enslaved or displaced communities, for refugee families, for those whose ancestors survived war, famine, or systemic violence.

And here is what is also true: generational healing is possible. The intention to heal can ripple backward and forward through a lineage. Setting that intention can itself bring up profound emotion. Prepare for it. Welcome it. It is the work.

Emotional Literacy: The Foundation of the Work

Many of the people you will support do not have a developed emotional vocabulary. They have been taught to push through feeling, to perform wellness, to manage the appearance of being okay.

Part of your role is to expand that vocabulary gently. To offer words. To widen the question. How are you feeling. And where do you feel that in your body. To make it safe to say I do not know what I am feeling as an honest and honoured answer.

Unpacking beliefs around emotions is also part of this work. Many people carry inherited messages that emotion is weakness. That vulnerability is dangerous. That certain emotions are shameful or inappropriate. These beliefs are protective. They were formed for good reason. Honour them even as you gently create space for something new.

Practices That Protect Your Capacity to Heal

- Regular supervision or consultation with a peer or mentor
- Personal therapy or your own healing practice, ongoing not occasional
- Clear transitions between client-facing work and personal time, a ritual that marks the boundary
- A **somatic** decompression practice after heavy sessions: shaking, stretching, cold water on the wrists
- Regular honesty with yourself about your current capacity
- A community of fellow practitioners who understand the weight of the work

Understanding trauma means understanding that every person in front of you is communicating through their nervous system before a single word is spoken. The responses you just learned to recognise, fight, flight, freeze, fawn, are the body's language. To receive that language, you need more than knowledge. You need **attunement**. What follows is the practice of learning to listen with your whole being, so that when the body speaks, you are present enough to hear it.

Attuning to Another Nervous System

Attunement is one of the oldest forms of human medicine. Before words. Before technique. Before any framework or certification, there was this: one person turning their full attention toward another and letting that attention be felt.

Attunement is the practice of tuning your own system to the frequency of another person's, the way you might adjust a dial until two signals begin to resonate. It is how infants learn that the world is safe. It is how **repair** happens in **rupture**. It is the invisible architecture beneath every genuine healing relationship. And it is a skill. It can be developed, refined, and practised until it becomes as natural as breathing.

What Attunement Actually Is

Attunement is sometimes confused with empathy, and while they are related, they are different in a precise and important way.

Empathy is the capacity to understand or feel what another person is experiencing. Attunement is the active, relational process of communicating that understanding back, in a way the other person's nervous system can actually receive.

You can feel deep empathy for someone in a private moment and never convey it. Attunement is empathy made visible through presence, pacing, and the quality of your attention. It is the difference between understanding someone's pain and that person feeling understood.

Stephen Porges' **polyvagal theory** gives us a framework for understanding why attunement works at the level it does. The social engagement system, the most recently evolved part of the autonomic nervous system, is specifically designed to read safety cues from other people. The tone of a voice, the softness around the eyes, the rhythm of a breath, the quality of stillness in a body: these are the signals it is constantly scanning for. When it detects them as safe, it opens. When it detects threat, it closes. Attunement is the practice of generating the cues that signal safety through that system.

Attuning Before You Speak

The first and most foundational act of attunement happens before a single word is exchanged. It happens in how you arrive. When you sit down with someone, take a breath and actually look at them. Let your eyes be soft. Let your face be open. Let your body be still in a way that communicates ease rather than vigilance. This is an act of intentional presence, and their nervous system reads it before their conscious mind does.

Many practitioners have been trained to fill the opening seconds of a session with welcomes, agendas, housekeeping. While structure matters, the most important thing you can do in those first moments is simply arrive, fully and visibly, in the room with another person. Let them see that you are here. Let your presence precede your words.

Matching Rhythm and Pace

Attunement involves a quality that researchers call **interactional synchrony**: the subtle mirroring of rhythm, pace, and movement that occurs between two people in genuine connection. You see it in people who are deeply engaged in conversation. Their gestures begin to mirror each other. Their breath begins to synchronize. Their speech rhythms converge.

This is something you can work with consciously.

If someone is speaking slowly and quietly, slow your own speech to meet them there before gradually, gently inviting them to a pace that allows more space. If someone is activated and speaking quickly, do not mirror the **activation**. Let your own slow, grounded pace become the invitation. The nervous system is highly responsive to vocal cues. Your steady rhythm is an anchor you are offering. Let them reach for it.

Pay attention to breath. When someone takes a visible breath, breathe with them. Not dramatically. Simply let your own breath move in accompaniment. This tiny act of synchrony communicates something that words rarely can: I am with you. I am here.

Tracking, the Felt Practice of Attuned Listening

Tracking is the somatic practice of following what is alive in another person's body and experience in real time, without interpretation, without agenda, simply following.

When you are truly tracking someone, you are attending to all the channels simultaneously: their words, their tone, their breath, their body, the feeling quality in the room. You are holding a kind of wide-lens attention that takes in everything at once without collapsing into analysis.

Tracking feels different from thinking about someone. Thinking about someone has a quality of mental effort, of processing, of evaluation. Tracking has a quality of presence. It is receptive. It is spacious. It requires that you slow your own internal activity down enough to actually feel what is happening in front of you.

Practitioners who have developed tracking say that it begins to feel like listening with the whole body. That they sense shifts in the person across from them before those shifts are visible. This is attunement working at its deepest level, the direct transmission of nervous system information between two people in genuine contact.

Following Before Leading

One of the most important principles in attuned facilitation is this: follow before you lead.

When you meet someone where they are first, in their pace, in their emotional register, in the quality of their current state, before attempting to guide them anywhere, you communicate something essential. You communicate that their current state is acceptable. That you are not trying to move them out of it. That they do not need to perform readiness or wellness in order to be valued in your space.

This is countercultural for many practitioners, who have been trained to create positive states, to move people toward insight, to generate momentum toward change. And while those things have their place, they belong later. First, you follow. First, you meet them wherever they are standing and let that place be enough.

Following sounds like: 'I am noticing a quietness in the room right now. I want to stay with that for a moment before we move forward.'

Following sounds like: sitting in a few seconds of silence after someone shares something heavy, rather than immediately responding.

Following sounds like: adjusting your entire plan for the session because the person in front of you needs something different from what you prepared and letting that adjustment be easy.

Naming What You Sense, Gently

Attuned practitioners sometimes name what they are sensing in the room, and this can be one of the most powerful relational moves available to you. It communicates that you are genuinely reading the person, that your attention is real, and that their internal experience is visible and honoured even when they have not spoken it aloud.

The key is to offer what you sense as a possibility, never a declaration.

'I am getting a sense that something shifted just then. I might be reading that wrong. How are you?'

'There is something I am noticing in the quality of your voice right now. I want to make sure I am not missing something. How are you feeling in your body?'

'Something feels tender in the room right now. Is that landing for you too?'

These offerings do several things. They model that bodies and energy are real and worth attending to. They demonstrate that you are genuinely present rather than running an agenda. And they create an opening for the person to name their own experience with less effort, because you have done the relational work of making the invisible visible first.

When Your Attunement is Off

You will misread people. You will follow a thread that was yours and lose theirs. You will offer a reflection that lands wrong. This is part of the practice.

When it happens, the repair is simple and it is part of the attunement itself. 'I want to check in. I may have misread something just now. How are you actually doing?' The willingness to be wrong and to ask again is itself an act of attunement. It communicates that their experience matters more than your interpretation of it.

Attunement is a practice of continual correction. A process of reaching, adjusting, reaching again. The goal is not perfect accuracy. The goal is genuine effort. And people feel the difference between a practitioner who is genuinely trying to find them and one who is performing the motions of care.

They always feel that difference. Their nervous system tells them.

CHAPTER TWO

The Everyday Witness

You did not sign up for this. And here you are. Sit down. Breathe. You are enough for this moment.

The Circle Is Widening

Something is changing in the world, and if you are reading this page, you can probably feel it. People are opening their mouths. The old silence that held so much grief and terror and unspoken inheritance is cracking. Children are telling their parents. Parents are telling their adult children. Partners are saying things that have been held for decades. Coworkers are shaking at their desks. Friends are texting at two in the morning.

The people being asked to listen, most of the time, are not therapists. They are not trauma specialists. They are the sister. The husband. The best friend. The auntie. The youth leader. The coworker who has always been the one people tell things to. They are you.

For a long time the teaching of how to hold another human being in their hardest moment was locked behind clinical training, behind certifications, behind degrees. That gate has not served us. The world needs a wider circle of witnesses, and the wider circle is already here. You are in it.

This chapter is for you. If you are a trained practitioner, it is also for you, because you were a friend, a sister, a son, or a coworker before you were a practitioner. The everyday witness lives inside you still.

What Witnessing Actually Is

Witnessing is the practice of staying. It is the act of being present with another human being while they feel something you cannot take away. It is refusing to look away. It is refusing to fix. It is refusing to rush. It is refusing to make their pain about you.

Witnessing is not therapy. You are not trying to heal them. You are not diagnosing. You are not interpreting. You are doing something older than any of those professions. You are the one who stays.

The human nervous system has always known this. When something terrible happens to a body, that body looks for another body. A soft voice. Steady breath. A hand. Eyes that do not flinch. The presence of one calm human can change what a nervous system is able to do with what it just lived through. This is called co-regulation, and it is the oldest medicine our species has.

You were born knowing how to do this. Life taught you to stop. Culture taught you to fix. The kindness of slowing down will bring you back.

Permission to Not Know

Before anything else, receive this: you do not need to know what to do. You will not have the right words. You will freeze sometimes. You will say something awkward. You will cry when you meant to be steady. You will be steady when you wished you could cry.

None of that is failure. All of it is the honest texture of being a human in the room with another human. The person across from you is looking for a person who did not leave. You can be that person whether or not the words come easily.

If you take only one thing from this chapter, take this: presence is more important than performance. A friend who sat with you in silence while you cried is remembered for a lifetime. A friend who said something brilliant is rarely remembered at all.

What Actually Happens in a Disclosure

When someone tells you something they have been carrying, their body is doing something brave. The story has often been sitting in their nervous system for years, held by protective structures, held by the parts of them that kept them functional. When they speak, those structures loosen. Old pain can rise. They may feel shaky, or nauseous, or suddenly cold. They may cry without knowing why. They may laugh at a moment that is not funny.

All of this is the body doing what the body was built to do. You are watching a nervous system metabolize what has been stored. Your job is to make the room safe enough for that metabolizing to happen.

You do not need to understand the body chemistry. You need to trust the body. It knows what it is doing. The body is producing a response that has always made sense.

The First Three Minutes

The first three minutes of a disclosure will shape what happens in the next three years. A person's body is reading you before their mouth has finished speaking. Your eyes, your shoulders, your breath, the quality of your silence: all of it is being received.

The first three minutes are not about what you say. They are about what you do not do.

What Not to Do in the First Three Minutes

- Do not gasp or recoil. The body across from you will read that as shock and recoil further.
- Do not immediately say what you would have done or what they should do.
- Do not ask for more details than they are offering. Their pace is the right pace.

- Do not start crying so hard that they have to comfort you. Some tears are a gift. Collapse is a burden.
- Do not reach for the explanation. Do not say it was meant to be, everything happens for a reason, what does not kill you makes you stronger, time heals, or any other sentence that moves them off the moment they are in.
- Do not rush to name who was wrong. You can witness the harm later. In this moment, just witness the person.

What to Do in the First Three Minutes

- Breathe. Long exhale. Your calm is contagious.
- Soften your eyes. Hardness reads as judgment even when you do not mean it.
- Let them finish a sentence. Most people finish what they started saying if the room is quiet enough.
- Say less than you want to say.
- Trust silence. Silence is presence without pressure.

Five Sentences That Almost Always Land

Everyday supporters often freeze because they do not know what to say. Here are five sentences that have landed for people in some of the hardest moments of their lives. They are simple on purpose. Simple is what nervous systems receive.

- Thank you for trusting me with this.
- I am here. I am not going anywhere.
- You do not have to explain more than you want to.
- I am so sorry that happened to you.
- I believe you.

Say one. Let it land. Do not pile all five on in one breath. Words spoken slowly reach a body. Words piled up become noise.

The Posture of the Body

Your body is as much part of the witness as your words. The nervous system in front of you is reading your body constantly, below any conversation. Consider:

- Sit at an angle rather than directly across. Direct opposition can read as confrontation to a system already on alert.
- Keep your hands visible and relaxed. Hidden hands signal threat to an old part of the brain.
- Match their posture softly. Slight mirroring is an ancient language of belonging.
- Slow your own breathing. Long exhales bring your system toward ventral vagal safety, and the body across from you is allowed to borrow your rhythm.
- Do not stand over them if they are seated. Match their height.
- If physical touch is wanted and welcome, offer it carefully. Ask first. For some trauma survivors, any touch will be too much. Their no is information.

Presence Is Attention, Not Silence

Silence alone is not enough. A silent witness who is mentally planning dinner is not really witnessing. Presence is the quality of attention you bring. Your whole body is listening. Your eyes are soft. Your breath is slow. You are letting what is being said actually land in you.

If you notice yourself drifting, come back to your feet on the floor. Come back to the sound of their voice. Come back to this breath. You can wander and return many times inside one conversation. The return is part of the practice.

What Fixing Does, and Why It Harms

Fixing is the reflex to end someone else's pain by solving it. It feels like love. It is often a form of self-soothing. When we rush to fix, we are managing our own distress about what we are hearing, rather than staying with what the other person actually needs.

Fixing says: your pain is too much for me. It says: your body cannot hold this, so let us skip to the part where it is over. It says: your process must match my tolerance.

The person disclosing does not need their pain solved in the moment of telling it. They need their pain received. The solving, when it comes, comes from their own body, in their own time, often days or weeks or months later. Your job is to keep the room warm while they find their way.

The Question That Saves You

What do you need right now?

When you do not know what to do, this question almost always points the way. You may not always get a clear answer. They may say I do not know. That answer is also a gift, because it tells you they do not need you to act yet. They need you to stay.

If they do name something, believe them. Sometimes they need a walk. Sometimes they need water. Sometimes they need you to leave the room so they can cry alone. Sometimes they need you to call their mother. Trust what they say, even when it is smaller than what you wanted to give.

When You Are Out of Your Depth

There will be moments when you are not the right support. The disclosure will contain something that needs a trained professional.

Active suicidality. Ongoing abuse. Severe dissociation that is not resolving. Trauma layered so deep that your presence is a drop in an ocean they need a lighthouse for.

In those moments, your job is still presence. You stay in the room. You do not abandon them because the help they need is bigger than you. And you gently, clearly open the door to the wider circle. You help them call a crisis line. You drive them to the hospital. You sit beside them while they text their therapist. You hold the space for a handoff.

Knowing your limits is a form of love. A river does not apologize for being a river and not an ocean. You are what you are, and you are bringing what you can bring. The wider circle is there for what you cannot.

Caring for Your Own System Afterward

A body that just witnessed something hard needs care too. Witnessing costs the body real resources. If you repeatedly witness without tending, your own system will begin to carry the weight. Everyday supporters are as susceptible to vicarious trauma as trained practitioners.

After a hard conversation:

- Move your body. Walk. Stretch. Shake your arms and legs. Discharge the activation that built up while you were still.
- Drink water. The body metabolizes emotion with water.
- Name what you witnessed to one other trusted human, without breaking confidence. I just held something heavy. Can you be with me for a few minutes?
- Feel your feet. Feel the ground. Look around the room. Orient to where you are.

- If the conversation was particularly intense, give yourself a full day of softer pace before stacking more demands on your system.

A witness who does not tend to themselves becomes a fountain with no source. The mission of being present to others asks you to be present to yourself first.

The Long Relationship

Most disclosures are not one-time events. Once a person has told you, the relationship is different. You have been trusted with something load-bearing. They may bring it up again. They may never bring it up again. They may pull away for a while, sometimes because the telling itself was overwhelming. They may circle back months later.

Your job in the long relationship is to keep the door open without pushing. Once in a while, you might say: I was thinking about you. I hold what you told me with care. I am still here. The body across from you will feel that and will return when they are ready, or not at all, and either answer is theirs to make.

A Short Practice Before a Hard Conversation

When you know a hard conversation is coming, and you have even a minute or two to prepare, try this:

- Feel your feet on the floor. Notice whatever is underneath them.
- Take three long exhales. Longer than the inhales.
- Put your hand on your own heart. Say silently: I am here. I am enough for this.
- Picture the person you will be sitting with. Send them a silent wish: may you feel met.
- Walk in.

This takes sixty seconds. It changes the nervous system you carry into the room. The person across from you will receive a different body because you did this.

A Blessing for the Everyday Witness

May you remember that your presence is ancient medicine. May you trust that staying is sometimes all the healing the moment can hold. May you know that when you do not have the right words, your breath is still speaking. You did not fail. You stayed. That is the beginning of everything.

CHAPTER THREE

The Nervous System Primer

The body is doing the job it has always done. Our work is to understand the job and stop fighting it.

Why a Primer

Much of what feels wrong inside a trauma response is actually the body doing exactly what it was built to do. The shaking. The freeze. The inability to remember words. The sudden panic in the grocery store. The numb flatness on the day everyone expected to be a good day. None of this is malfunction. All of it is architecture.

This chapter offers four maps. Together they give you a vocabulary for what is happening when a nervous system moves through the world. You do not need to memorize all of them. You need only to feel, by the end of this chapter, that the body has reasons. Once you sense the reasons, the fixing impulse softens. The witnessing opens.

The maps are the polyvagal ladder, the window of tolerance, the four F responses, and neuroception and glimmers.

Map One: The Polyvagal Ladder

Stephen Porges gave the world polyvagal theory. Deb Dana translated it into a teaching shape that the body can learn in an afternoon. She called it a ladder. Picture three rungs.

At the top of the ladder, the body is in ventral vagal state. This is safety and social engagement. You can look someone in the eye. You can speak and listen. You can feel your feet and your belly. You are open. Your breathing is easy. This is the state the body comes home to.

In the middle rung, the body is in sympathetic activation. The fight and flight system. Heart pounding. Muscles tight. Breath shallow. The body has decided there is a threat, and energy has been mobilized to meet it. This is the body being alert for you.

At the bottom rung, the body is in dorsal vagal shutdown. Frozen. Collapsed. Flat. Absent. This is the oldest response in the mammalian tree. When the body cannot fight and cannot flee, it plays dead. It slows everything down. This looks like depression, dissociation, numbness, chronic exhaustion, the inability to get off the couch.

A nervous system moves up and down this ladder all day. A healthy system can move. A system shaped by chronic trauma often gets stuck, spending long stretches in sympathetic activation or dorsal shutdown, with only brief visits to ventral safety.

When you watch someone in front of you, you are watching where they are on the ladder. The person in sympathetic is agitated, fast-talking, wide-eyed. The person in dorsal is flat, far away, hollow. The person in ventral can meet your eye and actually hear you. Your job as witness is to offer a ventral body so theirs has somewhere to climb back toward.

This is co-regulation. One ventral system lends safety to a system that cannot find it alone. It is the oldest medicine.

A Simple Practice for Finding Your Own Ladder

- Sit. Feet on the floor. Soft eyes.
- Notice your breath without changing it.
- Ask: where am I on the ladder right now?
- If you are in ventral, notice what ventral feels like in your body, so you can recognize it again.
- If you are in sympathetic, name it. Long exhales. Hum. Sigh. Move.

- If you are in dorsal, name it. Gentle movement. A cold drink. A slow walk. Sunlight. Do not push.

The first gift of the ladder is knowing where you are. The second gift is knowing that where you are now is not where you will be forever.

Map Two: The Window of Tolerance

Daniel Siegel gave us the window of tolerance. It is a simple image. Draw a horizontal line across a page. That is the floor of the window. Draw another horizontal line above it. That is the ceiling.

Inside the window, a person can feel, think, and engage. They can hold difficult emotions without being overwhelmed. They can receive and give. This is the zone where life is actually lived.

Above the ceiling is hyperarousal. Too much activation. Anxiety, panic, rage, overwhelm. The body has been pushed above its capacity to process.

Below the floor is hypoarousal. Too little activation. Numbness, collapse, shutdown. The body has dropped below its capacity to engage.

Trauma narrows the window. A person with a narrow window is pushed into hyperarousal or hypoarousal by things that would not shake another system. This is why someone you love may react to a small event in a way that seems disproportionate. Their window is narrower than yours. What you see as a small event is not small inside their system.

Healing is the widening of the window. Activation is part of being alive. Healing is the widening of what can be held inside it.

Signs Someone Is Above Their Window

- Fast talking, pressured speech.
- Trembling, sweating, racing heart.

- Anger that rises quickly.
- Difficulty focusing. Thoughts spinning.
- Feeling unsafe in their own skin.

Signs Someone Is Below Their Window

- Flat affect. Monotone voice.
- Slow movements. Heavy body.
- Difficulty answering questions.
- Disconnected gaze.
- Reports of feeling empty, numb, or far away.

How to Help Someone Return to Their Window

For someone above the window, the work is settling. Long exhales. Slow movement. Cool water. Quiet. A soft voice. Weight on the body, like a heavy blanket or a hand on the back. Presence without pressure.

For someone below the window, the work is activation. Gentle movement. Sunlight. Orienting to the room. Naming colours. A piece of chocolate. A cold washcloth on the face. Humming. A walk.

In both cases, the goal is not to fix the person. The goal is to invite the body back into its range.

Map Three: The Four F Responses

When the body perceives threat, it selects from a menu of survival responses. Pete Walker, building on generations of trauma work, named four. Fight. Flight. Freeze. Fawn. These have been named, and now you can find your own.

Fight is the mobilization to meet threat directly. Aggression. Anger. Confrontation. Raised voice. Clenched fists. The fight response in chronic form looks like the adult who is always ready for a battle.

Flight is the mobilization to escape. Running. Avoiding. Overworking. Keeping busy. Leaving relationships. The flight response in chronic form looks like the adult who cannot sit still, cannot rest, cannot stop moving.

Freeze is the immobilization response. Playing dead. Going blank. Being unable to move or speak. Dissociation. The freeze response in chronic form looks like the adult who regularly loses time, cannot make decisions, or feels far away from their own life.

Fawn is the response Walker named and that the field was slow to see. Appeasement. Pleasing. Making oneself small. Anticipating what the threat wants and offering it before being asked. The fawn response in chronic form looks like the adult who cannot say no, who dissolves their own needs in service of others, who feels most safe when they are giving.

Most people have a dominant F response that formed in childhood, shaped by what was available. A child cannot fight or flee their own caregivers. Freeze and fawn are often the child's only options. The adult who watched their mother fawn her way through an abusive partner may fawn in every adult relationship without knowing they are doing it. The adult who fought to survive a chaotic household may fight every partner who ever tries to love them.

Understanding your own dominant F response is some of the most useful self-knowledge a witness can carry. It tells you where your blind spots will be. A fawn-dominant witness may rush to make the discloser feel better to regulate their own discomfort. A flight-dominant witness may cut a conversation short because the intensity is unbearable. A freeze-dominant witness may dissociate during the telling and miss what was said. A fight-dominant witness may immediately decide who needs to be punished, running past the person who actually needs care.

Finding Your Own F Response

Ask yourself: when I am afraid, what does my body do first?

- Does it get loud, hot, and ready to push? That is fight.
- Does it get anxious, busy, and looking for a way out? That is flight.
- Does it go still, blank, and far away? That is freeze.
- Does it start scanning for what the other person wants so it can give it to them before they ask? That is fawn.

You probably have a primary response and a secondary response. Knowing both gives you a map of your own nervous system. It also gives you compassion for the nervous systems around you, each of whom is operating from their own set.

Map Four: Neuroception and Glimmers

Neuroception is the word Stephen Porges gave to something your body does constantly without telling you about it. Beneath conscious awareness, your nervous system is scanning every environment for cues of safety or danger. It reads faces, tones, postures, the quality of light in a room, the behaviour of strangers, the sound of footsteps. It decides, before you decide, whether to lean forward or pull back.

Trauma narrows and sharpens neuroception. A system shaped by threat reads danger in places where none exists. This is why a survivor may feel panicked in a completely safe room, or may react to a tone of voice that did not register for anyone else. Their system is doing its job based on what it has learned. The learning was necessary. It just is not always accurate anymore.

Understanding neuroception changes the witness. It lets you take a loved one's sudden shift in state at face value. Their body read something you did not read. Instead of arguing with their system, you can trust their system and help it update. What are you noticing? What does your body need right now?

Glimmers are neuroception's gift. Deb Dana named them. A glimmer is a micro-moment of safety the nervous system catches and registers. The warm light of a morning kitchen. A dog's paw in the lap. A friend's laugh. The smell of cedar. A song that always steadies the chest.

Glimmers are the raw material of healing. A nervous system that has been in chronic survival mode has often stopped noticing them. Part of recovery is training the attention back toward glimmers. Pointing them out. Collecting them. Stacking them until the body begins to expect them.

For the witness, glimmers are a teachable practice. Ask your loved one: what is a glimmer you had today? Watch their face change when they name one. You can offer your own. You can create glimmers for each other: the tea in a favourite cup, the particular playlist, the evening walk at the same time every week. Small, repeated, embodied invitations of safety.

Putting the Maps Together

You do not need to remember the names. You need to carry the underlying truth these maps point toward. The body makes sense. Every response it produces has a reason rooted in survival. When you see a loved one shaking, or dissociating, or fawning, or snapping, you are watching a nervous system doing what a nervous system does. Your work is to soften. To breathe. To be curious about what the body needs. To trust that the body, given safety and time, knows how to metabolize what has been carried.

And when you turn those same eyes on yourself, you find the same grace. You have been responding all along. Your responses were not evidence of weakness. They were evidence of aliveness. The body kept going. That is what the body is for.

PART TWO

The Inner Work of the Witness

• • •

Now we turn inward.

The first question is never what do I do for them. The first question is always what shape am I in when I arrive. What state is my nervous system in. What has gone unmetabolized in me this week, this year, this lifetime, that might reach for the story of the person in front of me. What practices live in my body that can bring me back when I drift.

These chapters walk you through the work no one sees. The sacred pre-work. The somatic practices that keep you open without making you porous. The moment mid-session when your own story gets activated and you need to know how to come home. The protection that does not harden you.

Read these slowly. Practice them before you need them. The reader who skips this part will burn out in the work. The reader who gives themselves to this part will find the work sustainable, generative, and deeply good.

CHAPTER FOUR

The Sacred Pre-Work: Before You Begin

Every powerful facilitation, one-on-one session, or team leading activity begins before the first person walks through the door. It begins with you.

Your Own Regulation Is the Foundation

You cannot offer a regulated nervous system to another person if your own is dysregulated. **Co-regulation**, the process by which one calm nervous system helps another find its way back to baseline, only works when one person in the room is actually regulated.

This is not about performing calm. Performing calm is its own kind of deception and people's nervous systems detect it. This is about genuinely arriving in your body, in your breath, in the present moment before you begin.

Before every session, ask yourself:

- What am I carrying today that is not mine to carry into this space?
- Where am I in my own **window of tolerance** right now?
- Have I eaten? Slept? Moved my body in a way that feels **grounding**?
- Is there anything unresolved between me and this person that I need to name or set aside?
- Am I showing up for them or am I showing up for how helping them makes me feel?

The Window of Tolerance

The window of tolerance describes the optimal zone of arousal in which a person can function effectively. Inside the window, we can think clearly, feel our feelings without being overwhelmed, and engage with others. Outside it, we are either hyper-aroused, in fight or flight, or hypo-aroused, in freeze or shutdown.

Know your own window. Know what expands it and what collapses it. Know your early warning signs that you are leaving it. Because if you leave your window during a session, your capacity to hold someone else diminishes significantly.

Vicarious Trauma and Compassion Fatigue

Witnessing pain is costly. Hearing stories of abuse, neglect, loss, and systemic harm changes you at a cellular level over time. This is a feature of your empathy, which is also your greatest gift. Treat it as information about what the work is asking of you.

Vicarious trauma refers to the cumulative impact of being repeatedly exposed to others' traumatic material. **Compassion fatigue** refers to the depletion that comes from giving care without adequate replenishment. Both are real. Both are common among healers. Both are preventable with intentional practice.

Knowing Your Scope Before You Begin

Every practitioner has a scope of practice, whether or not it is formally named. Your scope is the boundary of your training, your lived experience, your current capacity, and your ethical obligation to the people you serve.

Knowing your scope before you sit with someone means doing an honest assessment of what you are equipped to hold. Knowing your scope is how the service you offer stays genuinely safe. Scope is what keeps care from collapsing into harm. Chapter Nine provides a full scope assessment tool.

Setting Your Own Intention

Before every session, take a moment to set your intention. It can be as simple as a breath and a silent commitment: I am here to serve this person's highest good. I am not here to fix, perform, or manage. I am here to witness.

Power, History, and the Relational Field

Every helping relationship carries a power differential. Name this early. 'I am aware that I am in a facilitator's role in this space, and I want you to know that the power in this room belongs to you. My role is to offer structure and accompaniment. The direction always belongs to you.'

And then mean it. Every time. In every choice you make about pace, content, and direction.

When you are aware of safety and the impacts of trauma, you become very aware of how power has impacted people's lives. To embody a person with safe usage of power is one of the most healing acts of service any one of us can offer. It allows for modelling of what may have never been experienced by people you are supporting. Much of the experience of healing is in the process itself that is relational, rather than just the content shared and moved through. This means that when you are humble rather than authority driven, you are supporting their nervous system to regulate in your presence. You are embodying healthy power rather than one that is looking to just direct and have obedience. Many of us have been socially hardwired this way from things like familial belief systems, school systems, and cultural norms that treat young people as less competent and more needing to be obedient vs. autonomous. This creates a nervous system that is hardwired to comply rather than offer the opportunities to explore, learn and adapt to new ways of being. This is our role. To remind people they are sovereign beings having an experience to discover who they truly are beyond the conditioned norms that have told us to only listen and obey to not risk punishment, discipline, censorship, etc. We will always attach before we will risk not belonging and connecting and if attaching is conditional to behave a certain way, we will modify our behaviour and therefore adapt to become what is wanted of us, rather than what is genuine. Being in a healing role, means we are modelling that level of freedom, consent, and respect that is necessary for people to discover themselves for often the first time ever. If someone is embodied already it would be important that you are aware of your own need for control or you will likely get triggered by this.

Pre-Session Checklist

Environment

- ☐ Space is physically welcoming: lighting, seating, temperature
- ☐ Water and tissues are accessible and in view
- ☐ Restroom location has been communicated
- ☐ Distractions have been minimized
- ☐ There is a clear exit that does not require explanation

Practitioner Preparation

- ☐ I have checked in with my own nervous system and am within my window of tolerance
- ☐ I have set a clear intention for this session
- ☐ I have completed any somatic preparation: breath, movement, grounding
- ☐ I know my scope for this session and have a referral plan if needed

Opening Essentials

- ☐ Safer space agreements are prepared to co-create with participants
- ☐ Right to withdraw language is planned and will be stated clearly
- ☐ A grounding or arrival practice is prepared
- ☐ Session arc has been communicated: what, how long, what is available

Emergency Awareness

- ☐ I know what to do if someone becomes acutely distressed
- ☐ I have crisis resource information available

CHAPTER FIVE

Somatic and Grounding Practices: The How

This chapter gives you the actual tools. Not the concept of **grounding**. The grounding.

Throughout this book you have been invited to offer grounding practices and to use **somatic** tools in your own regulation. This chapter names them specifically so you can walk into any session with a clear repertoire. These are practices you can offer to clients and practices you can use yourself.

Learn them in your own body first. Practice them when you are regulated so they are available to you when you are not.

The 5-4-3-2-1 Orientation Practice

This is one of the most accessible and effective grounding tools available because it works through the senses, which are always present-moment anchors. It interrupts a stress response by directing attention outward, away from the internal spiral and back into the room.

How to Guide 5-4-3-2-1

- 'Let us slow down together for a moment. I am going to guide you through something simple.'
- 'Look around the room and find 5 things you can see. Name them, silently or aloud, whatever feels right.'
- 'Now find 4 things you can physically feel right now. The weight of your body in the seat. Your feet on the floor. The temperature of the air. The fabric of your clothes.'

- 'Now notice 3 things you can hear. They can be near or far.'
- 'Now 2 things you can smell. Or if there is nothing distinct, simply breathe in and notice the quality of the air.'
- 'And finally, 1 thing you can taste right now, or one thing you genuinely appreciate in this moment.'
- 'Take one breath. Notice where you are. You are here. You are okay.'

Shaking and Tremoring

Animals shake after a threatening experience and return naturally to equilibrium. Humans, having learned to suppress visible emotion, often inhibit this response. Intentional shaking is a way of completing the incomplete stress cycle in the body.

Peter Levine's somatic experiencing work and the Trauma Release Exercises developed by David Berceli both ground this practice in neuroscience. The tremor or shaking movement is the body's natural mechanism for discharging **activation** from the nervous system.

How to Guide Shaking

- Offer this as an option, never a requirement, particularly in group settings where it may feel vulnerable.
- 'If it feels okay, let your hands begin to shake gently. Just let them. Not performed. Just allowed.'
- 'You can let that move up your arms if it wants to. Some people find it moves through the whole body. There is nothing wrong with you if it does. That is your nervous system completing something.'
- 'Shake for thirty seconds to two minutes, then stop and be still. Notice what has shifted.'

- For practitioners using this for yourself: shake your hands and arms after a heavy session. Let your body discharge what it absorbed.

Bilateral Tapping

Bilateral stimulation, alternating sensory input between the left and right sides of the body, is the foundational mechanism behind EMDR therapy. Simple tapping practices accessible to any practitioner can draw on this principle to help resource and regulate the nervous system.

The **butterfly hug**, crossing the arms over the chest and alternating taps on the upper arms or shoulders, is one of the most widely used bilateral practices. It is gentle, self-contained, and can be done sitting without requiring any equipment or explanation of complex theory.

How to Guide the Butterfly Hug

- 'Cross your arms over your chest, right hand on your left shoulder or upper arm, left hand on your right.'
- 'Begin tapping alternately. Right, left, right, left. Slow and gentle. Like a heartbeat.'
- 'As you tap, bring to mind a resource: a place that feels safe, a memory of being held, a quality in yourself you trust. Let it be simple.'
- 'Continue for thirty seconds to two minutes, breathing gently.'
- 'When you stop, place both hands flat on your chest and feel the warmth. Take one breath.'
- You can also offer simple knee tapping: hands resting on the knees, alternating taps, same rhythm and intention.

Cold Water and Sensory Reset

Cold water on the wrists, face, or back of the neck activates the **mammalian dive reflex** and can produce a rapid shift in nervous system state. This is particularly useful for hyperarousal, when the system is flooded and needs to come down quickly.

For practitioners: keep water nearby and use it after heavy sessions. Wash your hands with intention. Let the temperature of the water be a signal to your nervous system that the session is complete and you are now tending to yourself.

The Physiological Sigh

Research from Stanford has identified the **physiological sigh**, a double inhale through the nose followed by a long exhale through the mouth, as the most efficient breath pattern for reducing physiological stress. The double inhale re-inflates the air sacs in the lungs and the long exhale activates the **parasympathetic nervous system**.

This takes five seconds. It is always available. It is something you can do invisibly in a session when you need to resource yourself without breaking the relational flow.

You are not just teaching grounding. You are modelling that the body is a resource. Every time you slow down and invite someone into their senses, you are teaching them that the body can be a place of return, not only a place of danger.

CHAPTER SIX

When YOU Get Triggered Mid-Session

This chapter exists because almost no one talks about it, and almost every practitioner has lived it.

You are in the middle of a session. The person across from you shares something. And something in you moves. Not toward them in empathy, but inward, toward your own story. Your chest tightens. Your mind narrows. Your words dry up. Or you go on autopilot, continuing to speak while something in you has quietly left the room.

This is you in a stress response. And it happens to every practitioner who has a nervous system, which is all of them.

What you do in that moment matters enormously. Not for the sake of appearing professional, but because the person in front of you deserves someone who is actually present, and you deserve to know how to return to yourself without abandoning the room.

Why This Happens

Practitioners are not separate from their history. The same nervous system that makes you empathetic and attuned is the same system that carries your own unprocessed experiences. When content in a session brushes up against one of your own unhealed places, your system responds. This is called countertransference in clinical language. In human language, it is called being a person.

Common triggers for practitioners include:

- Content that mirrors your own history or family system
- A relational dynamic in the room that replicates something from your past

- A particular emotion, like grief, rage, or helplessness, that is unresolved in you
- A client who reminds you of someone significant in your life
- The weight of cumulative exposure to pain across many sessions
- Feeling helpless or out of your depth, which may link to earlier experiences of powerlessness

Recognizing It in Real Time

The first skill is noticing. This requires a degree of self-awareness that is built over time with practice. In the moment, your indicators may include:

- A physical sensation: chest tightening, throat closing, heat rising, stomach dropping
- A sudden blankness or inability to track what the person is saying
- A strong emotional response that feels slightly out of proportion to the moment
- An urge to redirect the conversation, fill the silence, or rush through what is surfacing
- Feeling suddenly very focused on the technique, the next question, the agenda, rather than the person
- A quality of disconnection, going through the motions while something in you is elsewhere

The In-the-Moment Protocol

When you notice you have been triggered, you have a few seconds to make a choice. Here is a simple four-step protocol:

P.A.C.E. for When You Are Triggered

P: Pause

Internally. You do not need to pause the session visibly. Take one breath and let it be slightly longer than your last one. This breath is for you.

A: Acknowledge

Name it to yourself, silently. 'I have been activated.' Witness yourself the same way you would witness a client. The noticing itself is the practice.

C: Contain

Gently set your own material to the side. Not permanently. Not with shame. Simply with an internal gesture: I see this. I will return to it. Right now, this person needs me here.

E: Engage

Return your full attention to the person. If you need a moment, use a tool: offer them a **grounding** practice, pour water, ask them to take a breath. This gives you thirty seconds to re-anchor before speaking.

When to Name It and When Not To

There are moments where naming your own response to a client is appropriate, deepens trust, and models the very humanness you want to create space for. There are also moments where bringing your material into the room is not in service of them.

A guideline: name it if it serves them, contain it if it is yours to process elsewhere.

If you choose to name it, keep it brief and redirect quickly. 'What you just shared touched something in me. I want to hold that for myself and make sure this space stays about you. Are you okay to continue?'

After the Session: Processing What Came Up

Whatever was activated in you during the session deserves attention after. Not in a spiral of self-criticism, but with the same gentle curiosity you would offer a client.

- Write down what surfaced and what it connected to in your own history
- Bring it to supervision or peer consultation as soon as possible
- Consider whether this content points to something that needs attention in your own healing work
- Notice if this practitioner-client pairing is consistently activating. That is important information.
- Be honest with yourself about whether you are currently resourced enough to continue working with this person

Being triggered does not make you a bad practitioner. It makes you a human practitioner. The question is not whether it will happen. It is whether you have a practice for when it does. Now you do.

CHAPTER SEVEN

Nervous System Protection Toolkit

This chapter belongs to you as a practitioner. It is a collection of specific, evidence-based tools for listening to trauma without carrying it.

Vicarious trauma is real. It is the psychological, emotional, and physiological impact that occurs when a person is repeatedly exposed to the traumatic experiences of others, especially through listening to detailed accounts of suffering, violence, or harm. It most often affects people in exactly the roles you hold: coaches, healers, facilitators, advocates, community helpers.

Listening to the experiences of others can be meaningful and necessary work. It can also hollow you out if you approach it without protection. These tools are your armour. Not the traum-our kind that shuts you down. The kind that keeps you open.

1. Regulated Breathing

What it is

- Slow, intentional breathing to calm the nervous system while remaining present and open.
- In practice
- Inhale for 4 counts
- Exhale for 6 to 8 counts
- You can do this invisibly while listening. No one needs to know.
- The longer exhale is the key: it is what activates the **parasympathetic nervous system**

Why it works

Longer exhales activate the rest-and-digest response and support emotional regulation without requiring you to exit the relational field. This is a tool you can use in real time, in session, without interruption.

2. Sensory Grounding

What it is

- Using sensory awareness to remain connected to the present moment while hearing distressing information.
- In practice
- Feel your feet on the ground
- Notice your body in the chair
- Hold a textured object in your hand
- Name objects in the room silently as you listen

Why it works

Grounding helps maintain present-moment awareness and reduces emotional overwhelm. It anchors you in the here and now so the person's story does not pull you entirely into their there and then.

3. Somatic Boundaries

What it is

- Maintaining a conscious psychological boundary while listening to difficult experiences.
- In practice
- Imagine a membrane or boundary at the edge of your body that allows empathy to pass through but not the story itself

- Visualize information arriving at you rather than entering you
- Place one hand gently on your own chest or leg as a subtle anchor to your own body

Why it works

This practice maintains empathy while preventing emotional merging with the person sharing. You can be moved without being swept away. Compassion does not require absorption.

4. Environmental Orientation

What it is

- Staying aware of the current physical environment while hearing traumatic material.
- In practice
- Periodically notice objects in the room around you
- Feel the support of your chair beneath you
- Look around gently when there is a pause, letting your eyes rest on something neutral

Why it works

Orienting to the environment signals safety to your brain and prevents emotional immersion in the trauma narrative. Your nervous system needs reminders that you are in a safe present, not inside the person's past.

5. Micro-Movement Release

What it is

- Small physical movements that release nervous system **activation** before it accumulates.
- In practice

- Roll your shoulders gently
- Stretch your hands and fingers
- Press your feet into the floor briefly and release
- Take one slow breath and let the exhale be audible if you are alone

Why it works

Trauma activates fight-or-flight energy. That energy needs physical discharge. Micro-movements allow you to release small amounts of activation as they build rather than carrying the whole session's accumulation in your body until the end.

6. Compassion Without Absorption

What it is

- Maintaining empathy while consciously recognizing that the trauma belongs to the other person.
- In practice
- Silently remind yourself: 'This story belongs to them.'
- 'My role is to witness, not to carry.'
- 'I can be present with their pain without making it mine.'
- After sessions, actively name what you are handing back: 'This is yours to heal. I am here to accompany you in that.'

Why it works

This prevents emotional fusion and reduces the risk of secondary traumatic stress. You are not less caring because you do not absorb. You are more sustainable. And sustainability is what allows you to keep showing up.

7. Sensory Reset After Exposure

What it is

- Intentional sensory experiences used after hearing traumatic stories to signal completion and return to your own baseline.
- In practice
- Step outside and feel the air
- Drink water or tea slowly and with attention
- Wash your hands or face with intentional presence
- Shake your hands and arms
- Place both hands on your chest for a full breath

Why it works

This helps your nervous system understand that the listening is complete and you are now returning to your own life. Without this signal, the body can continue to process the session's content long after it has ended, contributing to vicarious trauma over time.

You are allowed to protect yourself. In fact, you are required to. A healer who has absorbed what was never theirs to carry cannot offer the presence the work requires. Protection is not distance. It is how you stay.

PART THREE

Meeting Those Who May Live Unique to Our Own Lived Reality

• • •

Now we turn outward.

You will not sit with a generic human. You will sit with a specific person, shaped by a specific history, carried in a specific body, standing at a specific intersection of culture, identity, and inherited story.

These chapters widen the lens. Treat them as preparation. So you can arrive with the humility to meet whoever actually walks through the door, with enough awareness to recognize what they might be carrying, and with enough care to honour the lineages inside their body.

The person in front of you is always more than any category. These chapters help you see the category clearly so you can see past it, to them.

CHAPTER EIGHT

Cultural Competency and Unique Ways of Knowing

Cultural competency is not a destination. It is a lifelong orientation of curiosity, humility, and respect.

Honouring Diverse Ways of Knowing

Western approaches to trauma and healing are not universal. They are one set of answers to a deeply human set of questions. Many Indigenous, African, Asian, Latin American, and other cultural traditions have their own rich frameworks for understanding suffering, resilience, and healing, and those frameworks often predate Western psychology by centuries.

When you encounter a person who understands their experience through a different lens than yours, through their own cultural lens, **ceremony**, through collective healing, through spiritual practice, through ancestral connection, your role is not to translate their experience into your framework. Your role is to hold your own framework loosely and be genuinely curious about theirs. They will process and identify what they are experiencing with the context and associations that are housed within their cultural paradigm. This is beautiful. This is sacred and cultural safety is very much woven with trauma-informed practices. Hundreds of ways of being exist. We all hold the stories of our ancestors and it's a gift to share space with those who have ancestors unique to us.

Ceremony, Plant Medicine, and the Sacred Responsibility of Preparation

Across cultures and throughout human history, ceremony has been a vessel for transformation. Sweat lodges, vision quests, breathwork journeys, plant medicine ceremonies, and sacred ritual of all kinds exist because humans have always known that healing sometimes requires crossing a threshold into an altered state of consciousness. These practices are ancient. They are powerful. And they are, for many people, profoundly effective at untangling layers of pain that conventional approaches have not reached.

This book does not prescribe or endorse any specific ceremonial practice. What it does is name something that anyone who supports people through these experiences must understand: the quality of what happens before and after ceremony is as important as the ceremony itself.

Plant medicines and other consciousness-expanding practices work by opening what has been held beneath the surface. They bring forward sensation, memory, grief, terror, and joy from the subconscious. They unravel layers of protection that the nervous system built over years, sometimes generations. For someone whose parents and grandparents never had the opportunity to process their own pain, for someone carrying centuries of compounded emotional inheritance in a world that has feared and avoided emotional expression, what surfaces during ceremony can be immense.

This is where trauma-informed awareness becomes essential.

A person entering ceremony needs a landing pad. They need to be witnessed and known beforehand. They need someone who can mirror back to them who they are in their wholeness, in their regulated state, in their capital-S Self, before they enter a process that will, by design, dissolve the familiar structures of identity and protection.

Many traditional medicine carriers have this capacity naturally. They can see where a person is in their authentic self and what has burdened them or pulled them from that centre. This is a gift cultivated across generations of practice, prayer, and deep **attunement** to the human spirit. It is a way of seeing that predates any clinical framework.

What this book offers is the complementary lens. The ability to recognize what stage of the journey someone is in. The language for what the nervous system is doing when someone is activated. The awareness to identify a **fight response**, a **freeze response**, a **fawn response** in the room. The **grounding** skills to support someone whose system is flooded. The capacity to hold steady when what is surfacing is bigger than words.

Because here is what can happen when preparation and **aftercare** are absent: a person goes through a powerful ceremonial experience, everything rises, everything rearranges, and then they return to a world that does not know how to hold what they have just moved through. They are left in the in-between. They have touched something true and raw and sacred, and there is no one on the other side to help them integrate what happened. No one to say: I see you. I saw you before, and I see you now. You are still here.

Integration is where healing becomes real. Without it, ceremony can open doors that leave people wandering through rooms they were never meant to enter alone.

If you are someone who supports people before, during, or after ceremony of any kind, every chapter in this book is relevant to your work. The nervous system does not distinguish between a therapy session and a ceremonial space. **Activation** is activation. **Dissociation** is dissociation. The need for safety, for a regulated presence, for someone who can hold the **container** while the process does its work: these are universal.

The people drawn to this path are often people who want to see a better world. They want to be part of that change. They carry hope and courage and a willingness to face what most people spend their lives avoiding. Honour that. And hold the understanding that foundational inner work, the slow and steady kind, the kind that builds a relationship with oneself before dissolving the known, is what allows ceremony to do its deepest work without leaving someone untethered.

You are the riverbank. Before, during, and after. Steady, solid, present. And because the riverbank holds, the water can move.

When You Do Not Know: The Practice of Asking

Not knowing is not a weakness. Pretending to know when you do not is.

'I want to make sure I am supporting you in a way that actually works for you. Are there things about how you understand healing or wellness that you would want me to know?' This question returns the authority for their care to the person receiving it, signals that your knowledge has limits, and opens a conversation that can fundamentally reshape how you show up.

Encouraging Inclusion Without Performing It

Inclusion is a practice, and it lives in the small choices you make every time you hold space. It is less about the words on a poster and more about how the room actually feels to the person standing at its edges. Here is what that looks like in practice:

- Using language that does not assume a shared cultural or religious background
- Offering multiple ways to participate that do not privilege verbal processing as the gold standard
- Asking about the person's preferences rather than assuming your way is the way

- Not requiring people to educate you as a condition of receiving care
- Acknowledging systemic barriers without making the individual responsible for fixing your understanding

When Healing Spaces Gaslight

Gaslighting in healing spaces rarely arrives with malice. It arrives wearing compassion. It sounds like reframes offered too quickly, like spiritual explanations layered over someone's lived pain before that pain has been witnessed on its own terms. It sounds like "everything happens for a reason" spoken to a person who has not yet been allowed to say what happened at all.

At its core, gaslighting is the act of making someone question the validity of their own experience. In therapeutic or healing contexts, it can look like a practitioner redirecting a client away from what they feel and toward what the practitioner believes they should feel. It can look like suggesting that distress is resistance, that anger is unprocessed ego, or that grief is a failure to surrender. It can look like centering a framework over a person.

This is different from offering perspective. Perspective is an invitation extended after someone's experience has been fully received. Gaslighting skips the receiving. It moves straight to correction.

Here are some of the ways it shows up in practice:

Reframing before witnessing. The client shares something painful. The practitioner immediately offers a positive reframe, a lesson, or a spiritual interpretation. The client's felt experience is bypassed before it is honoured.

Pathologizing emotional responses. A client's anger, grief, or shutdown is treated as a symptom to manage rather than a signal to listen to. The practitioner labels the response rather than being present with the human having it.

Implying the client is the problem. Language like "you're resisting the process" or "this wouldn't affect you if you had done the inner work" places the burden of the practitioner's discomfort onto the client. The client learns to distrust their own responses.

Using spiritual or holistic language to override **autonomy**. "Your higher self chose this experience" or "your body is holding onto this because you won't let go" are statements that can silence someone who is trying to speak their truth. These phrases can become tools of control when spoken from a position of authority.

The common thread in all of these is the same: the person's lived experience is overwritten by someone else's interpretation. The **felt sense** of the body is dismissed in favour of the practitioner's framework. And because it comes from someone the client trusts, the impact is compounded.

This matters because it leads directly to one of the most important distinctions in trauma-informed care: the difference between witnessing someone's pain and pathologizing it.

What Pathologizing Is and What It Is Not

Pathologizing means treating a normal human response as a disorder or deficiency. It sounds like: 'You seem to have real issues with trust.' Or: 'That sounds like an attachment disorder.'

Trauma-informed practice sounds like: 'Trust is something that gets shaped by our experiences. It makes sense that yours has been shaped the way it has.'

You are not a clinician. You are not here to diagnose. You are here to witness, accompany, and facilitate. Hold that lane.

Holding the Whole: Where Witnessing Meets Discernment

Everything we have explored in this chapter circles the same sacred ground: the space between someone's lived experience and what we, as practitioners, do with it.

Gaslighting dismisses the experience. Pathologizing reduces it to a label. Both remove the person from the centre of their own story. Both replace their knowing with ours. And both, in healing spaces, often happen with the best of intentions.

So where does that leave us?

It leaves us in the place that matters most: the practice of holding someone's experience as real, as worthy of being received, while also understanding that human beings make meaning. We interpret. We build stories from fragments of sensation, memory, belief, and pain. This is one of our most powerful capacities. It is also one of the places where suffering can quietly deepen.

A person's feelings are sovereign. Full stop. If someone feels unsafe, dismissed, unseen, that feeling is real and it deserves to be honoured without hesitation. The body does not lie about what it carries.

The interpretations that rise from those feelings, the stories we tell ourselves about why we feel what we feel, who is responsible, what it means, those are a different layer. They are real too. They matter. And they are also, by their nature, shaped by the lens through which we see the world. By our histories. By our **traum-our**. By the nervous system patterns that were once survival and have since become identity.

This is where the practitioner's presence becomes everything.

To hold someone's experience as valid while gently, slowly, with full permission, helping them explore the interpretations they have built around it: this is the heart of trauma-informed witnessing. It requires us to resist two opposing impulses at once. The impulse to correct ("that's just your perception") and the impulse to collude ("yes, and everyone else is the problem"). Neither serves the person. Neither honours their full humanity.

What serves the person is companionship in the inquiry. The willingness to say: "What you feel is real. I am here for all of it. And when you are ready, we can look together at the meaning you have made, with curiosity, with tenderness, and with your hand on the steering wheel the entire time."

The person always leads that exploration. Always. The moment a practitioner decides for someone what their experience means, whether that decision is a diagnosis, a spiritual reframe, or a well-meaning challenge, the power has shifted out of the client's hands. And that shift, no matter how subtle, is a departure from the sacred trust of this work.

Feelings are sovereign. Interpretations are explorable. The person leads. The practitioner witnesses.

This is the posture of **healership**. To be present enough to hold what is, wise enough to sense what is being carried beneath it, and humble enough to let the person unfold their own understanding in their own time.

CHAPTER NINE

People With Particularities That May Be Unique To You

Every group of people named is someone's whole life. This chapter is not a checklist. It is a series of doorways, each worth walking through slowly.

Weaving a Tapestry of Diversity and Unity

Trauma-informed practice begins with knowing your own position in the room. Who you are. What body you walk in. Which histories your body carries and which it does not. How you are spaced within the space and how you stand relationally with all peoples. Positionality is the first instrument of the work. Without it, the rest is unreliable.

Diversity is sacred. Every person is sacred. The room that forgets this becomes the room that does harm.

Then the truth has to be named. White Eurocentric values have been positioned as the superior way to be across nearly every sphere on earth. Beauty standards socially conditioned to privilege one kind of face. Productivity standards that reward one shape of output over rest and relationship. Thought processes held up as elite and standardized while other ways of knowing were dismissed as primitive. Even healing. Even the path to self-acceptance. All of it has been shaped by a single measuring stick that someone chose to call normal.

The route to feeling safe is not the same for everyone. It is not the same across origin stories. It is not the same within them. Two people of the same heritage may need entirely different things in the room. The assumption of shared experience inside a shared category is still a form of flattening.

This is why a trauma-informed way of being is always humble and reflexive. It knows itself. It asks questions of itself. It updates.

The same applies to every location outside the named centre. Those who are not able-bodied. Those who are not heterosexual or cisgender. Those whose stories are not named inside white spaces or inside white realities. The measuring stick for normal is arbitrary, and it maintains the dominance narrative any time the one holding it gets to define what life and its experience are meant to be about.

What follows names a few of the racialized locations the field has been slow to see clearly. A beginning.

The Indigenous Body

Indigenous peoples across every continent have been forced to live inside a world that is not their cultural set of truths. The attempted erasure was systemic and it was global. Language, ceremony, child-rearing practices, medicine, and relationship to land were all named as problems to be corrected. The child was taken, the language punished, the ceremony outlawed, the medicine driven underground.

Colonial harm has a specific weight in the Indigenous body. The severing lives in the nervous system across generations, and it is still arriving.

That weight lands inside a world whose default values are white, Western, and colonial. The healing frameworks most often offered were built outside Indigenous cosmologies and sometimes against them. The room itself can carry the epistemology that did the harm.

Their way of being, knowing, and meeting the space is medicine. It does not need translation. Hold your space with enough humility that the person does not have to explain, justify, or name themselves to be met.

Never other the person in front of you. Do not position your role as "allowing" them to be who they are. Allowing is a dominance word dressed in kindness. The person does not need your permission. Your job is to make the room safe enough that they never have to ask for it.

Racialized Trauma as a Category the Body Recognizes

Resmaa Menakem's contribution to the field has been to name racialized trauma as a somatic reality. The body of a person living under chronic racialization carries a specific pattern of nervous system activation. Constant low-grade hypervigilance. A readiness for insult or threat that most people in the dominant culture do not carry. Microaggressions lodging in tissue. Macroaggressions leaving marks across generations.

Menakem uses the term white body supremacy to describe the inherited somatic pattern that privileges certain bodies and threatens others. He teaches that healing racialized trauma requires settling the body first, before the mind can even begin the conversation. This is a somatic teaching. It meets the injury where it actually lives.

The Black Body and Specific Somatic Inheritance

The Black body in North America carries an inheritance that includes slavery, Jim Crow, redlining, mass incarceration, police violence, and ongoing medical neglect. The nervous system of a person raised in a Black body inherits their own lived experiences and the embodied memory of generations before them.

- Encounters with police are often trauma events even when uneventful on the surface.
- The medical system has a documented pattern of dismissing Black pain, particularly Black women's pain.
- Respectability politics is an exhausting and often invisible load.
- Code-switching is a form of labour the dominant culture does not see.
- The Black community has deep, ancestral practices of collective healing. Witnessing a Black client often includes making space for collective forms of care.

The Asian Diaspora

Asian diasporic clients carry a particular set of trauma patterns that the field has been slow to name. The pressure of the model minority myth. The silencing of emotional disclosure inside families. The trauma of war, refugee displacement, and intergenerational silence. The specific racialization that has intensified during and after the pandemic years.

- Emotional disclosure may come sideways, through somatic complaints, through caring actions, through food.
- The honouring of parents and elders can make it difficult for a survivor to name harms that occurred inside the family.
- The trauma of migration often includes the loss of a whole community, a whole language, a whole sensory world.
- Internalized perfectionism is often a survival strategy rooted in generational pressure.

The Latinx Experience

The Latinx client may carry trauma that includes migration, the border as a somatic threat, language loss across generations, machismo's particular pressures on men and women both, and the weight of Catholic religious structures. The current political moment in the United States is re-traumatizing for communities that have lived in fear of deportation and family separation for decades.

- The fear of ICE is not paranoia. It is reality-based and embodied.
- Mixed-status families carry a specific and constant nervous system load.
- Faith and family are often central to healing resources. Walk alongside rather than alternative to those resources.
- The pressure to be successful on behalf of a whole family, a whole lineage, a whole migration story is real, and rarely named.

South Asian Clients

- Speaking outside the family is often itself treated as a betrayal. A survivor who confides in you may be crossing lines that carry real consequences.
- Mental health language may be absent from the family vocabulary. Somatic language may be the only available articulation.
- Colourism, within the community, affects self-worth in ways the dominant culture does not see.
- Generational trauma from Partition, colonization, or war is carried in bodies even when never spoken.

The Refugee and Immigrant Body

A person who has left one country and rebuilt in another carries a nervous system that has been asked to do an enormous amount. The loss of a homeland. The loss of a language community. The grief of leaving family. The trauma of the journey itself.

- The body may carry trauma from the country of origin, trauma from the journey, and trauma from the receiving country. These stack.
- Children of immigrants often carry parentification patterns. This has a long nervous system cost.
- Assimilation pressure asks the body to disappear aspects of itself that were once survival. The reversal of this pressure is its own work of reclamation.
- For refugees from currently active conflicts, the news itself is retraumatizing.

Mixed Identity and the Grief of Not Fitting One Circle

Many clients belong to more than one community and fully belong to none. The Métis experience is one such location. The biracial experience is another. The child of immigrants who is neither wholly of the culture of origin nor wholly of the receiving culture. The transracial adoptee.

These clients often carry a specific grief of unbelonging. The feeling of being too much for one circle and not enough for another. The work of reclaiming a mixed identity as its own whole, rather than a broken half of two other things, is part of the healing.

Across Any Disclosure

Disclosures come into rooms held by people across every racial location. The person witnessing may carry the story in their own body, or may be meeting it from a different seat. Both positions matter. Both require care, of the client and of the self. What follows holds both.

When the story is not one you have lived in your body:

- Believe the description of what happened, even when it does not match your own experience of the world.
- Do not make the conversation about your own education. Your client is not your teacher. Do your own reading elsewhere.
- Do not perform guilt. Hold your own discomfort in your own body.
- Ask what they need. The answer will be specific to them.
- Acknowledge that you may have been a source of racialized harm at some point, however unintentionally. Leave the door open without insisting on opening it yourself.
- Respect that some of the healing your client needs will happen in spaces you are not part of. Let them go to those spaces without taking it personally.

When the story is one your body already knows:

- Your nervous system will often recognize the story before your mind catches up. Let that be information. You are not required to perform distance from your own knowing.
- Witnessing someone move through what you have moved through can reactivate your own pattern. Tend to yourself during, and tend to yourself after.
- You do not owe your client your whole story as proof of solidarity. A nod, a small word, a shared breath can be enough. Let them lead what they want to receive.
- Your own lineage of survival is medicine in the room. It does not have to be named to be felt.
- Be careful of the assumption that your experience and theirs are the same. Shared racialization does not mean shared story. Each body carries its own version.
- Your capacity to care for your own people is sacred. Protect it. Do not let it become obligation that drains you dry.

For every witness, regardless of the seat you are in:

The sacred witness is the sacred witness. The seat you sit in shapes what you bring. It does not decide whether you are capable of holding the room. Your lineage, your location, your own lived or unlived version of the story, all of it becomes part of the ground you offer. The work is to know your seat clearly, tend to yourself from it, and let the person in front of you be the author of their own story.

The Humility of the Word Humility

Cultural humility means something specific. It is not cultural competence (the idea that one can become fully skilled in another's culture). It is the ongoing posture of learning, of not-knowing, of letting the person in front of you be the authority on their own experience. It is lifelong. It does not graduate.

The facilitator who carries cultural humility has given up the comfort of feeling expert. In exchange, they have gained the capacity to actually see the person in front of them, rather than the category the culture taught them to see. This is the ground of the work.

That is the **sacred witness**.

LGBTQ2S+ Clients

Queer and trans clients carry what researchers call minority stress: the chronic, cumulative nervous system load of living in a society that treats their existence as contested. This is documented in health outcomes, in sleep quality, in rates of depression and anxiety, in the specific somatic signature of bodies that have been vigilant for years or decades.

What to hold as a facilitator:

- Coming out is not a single event. It is a lifelong series of decisions in individual situations. Each one costs something.
- Family rejection, even in subtle forms, is not processed quickly. It becomes part of the body.
- For trans clients, medical gatekeeping, legislative threat, and everyday vigilance (bathrooms, pronouns, paperwork) are ongoing stressors, not past ones.
- The risk of violence, particularly for trans women of colour, is real and well-documented.
- Two-Spirit identity, within Indigenous contexts, carries a distinct history of both honouring in pre-colonial times and suppression under colonial structures. A Two-Spirit client is carrying a story that is about gender, sexuality, and the reclaiming of an Indigenous tradition at the same time.

What queer and trans clients often report landing well: being believed, protected, and celebrated. Tolerance and acceptance are not enough. Celebration is the posture the body receives as true safety. This is a report that comes through from many voices, but it is always best practice to witness each individual as a person first and check in with them how they feel about identity and land there with them.

Neurodivergent Clients

Autistic clients, ADHD clients, dyslexic clients, and clients with sensory processing differences often experience their own bodies as misread. Many are diagnosed late. Many were told, for years, that they were broken versions of neurotypical when they were always whole versions of themselves.

The overlap between trauma and neurodivergence is now well-documented. Autistic masking, the performance of neurotypicality to be accepted, has trauma consequences. Rejection sensitive dysphoria in some ADHD bodies is real. Sensory overwhelm is a nervous system reaching a threshold the neurotypical world rarely considers.

As a facilitator:

- Sensory environments matter. Loud rooms, fluorescent lights, crowded spaces, scratchy fabrics may be actual pain.
- Meltdowns and shutdowns are nervous system events, not tantrums or attitude.
- Routines are often nervous system supports, not rigidity.
- Time blindness in ADHD is a real phenomenon, not disrespect.
- Late diagnosis can bring enormous grief for the years of being told you were the problem. Hold that grief with care.
- Many neurodivergent clients mask heavily in mainstream spaces and unmask only around those they trust. If a client unmasks with you, receive it as a gift.

Men as Trauma Survivors

Men often disclose less. Men often disclose later. Men often disclose in different idioms. The modern culture of late still teaches many men to equate emotional honesty with weakness, and the nervous system pattern that results is its own signature.

When a man is beginning to disclose in your space:

- The first disclosure may come through anger, through physical symptoms, or through behaviour changes, before it ever comes through words.
- Men who were sexually abused as children are one of the most silenced survivor populations. Up to one in six men in North America is a survivor of childhood sexual abuse, and the silence is almost absolute. A man disclosing this to you may be the first person he has ever told.
- Men in abusive relationships are similarly invisible in the literature and the culture. They may face doubt, mockery, or disbelief when they disclose.
- Men who come to the healing path often feel they are betraying their fathers, their grandfathers, or their lineage by speaking what was never spoken. Honour that weight.
- Tears from a man who has not cried in thirty years are sacred.

Women as Trauma Survivors

Women survive trauma in a particular context. The data on gender-based violence is staggering and has not meaningfully improved in a generation. One in three women in Canada will experience sexual violence in her lifetime. One in four women will experience intimate partner violence. Rates for Indigenous women, women with disabilities, and trans women are substantially higher. These are not distant statistics. They describe the women in every room you will ever hold.

When a woman comes to your space carrying trauma, she is almost always also carrying the ongoing work of holding other people. She is often the one who has held her children, her partner, her aging parents, her friends, her colleagues, her community. The space in which she finally speaks may be the first space in her life that belongs to her alone. Understand what it means that she chose you to give it to.

Things to hold as a witness to women survivors:

- Minimization is the dominant cultural response to women's pain. Most women have been told, in some form, that what happened was not that bad. They arrive with an internalized voice that shrinks their own experience before it reaches you. Your job is to refuse to shrink with them.
- Hypervigilance is often the signature. Women who have lived with threat, whether domestic, workplace, or street-level, have nervous systems that scan rooms. This is a body that learned, and the learning was intelligent. What presents as anxious personality is hypervigilance built into tissue by lived threat.
- Coercive control is a pattern that does not require physical violence to be devastating. Isolation. Financial control. Surveillance. The slow erosion of a person's sense of their own reality. Many women who have survived coercive control struggle to name what happened because there was no single event big enough to call abuse. Believe her anyway. What she survived is real whether or not the culture has words for it yet.
- Reproductive and maternal trauma is often unspoken. Birth trauma. Miscarriage. Stillbirth. Reproductive coercion. Forced sterilization, historically inflicted on Indigenous, Black, and disabled women in this country. Abortion grief. Infertility grief. Many of these losses do not receive the rituals they would in other cultures. A woman may arrive carrying a grief that has never been named as grief.

- Lateral violence among women, and between women, is real. The pressure to compete, to judge each other's choices, to enforce appearance and behaviour norms. Many women have been hurt by other women as much as by men. Hold that truth without flinching.
- The strong woman narrative is its own kind of trap. Women who have held everything for everyone often arrive unable to let themselves collapse. Give them permission, without pushing, to stop being strong in your presence. Permission is sometimes all a body needs to finally rest.
- When a woman's body has carried violence for years, it is almost never metabolized by the time she arrives. Much of it is still in the tissue. Witness slowly. Do not rush the body that is finally setting a burden down.

Brain Injury: A Hidden Layer in the Trauma Story

There is a layer to trauma work that almost no one names, and it is one of the reasons so many survivors feel misread. Brain injury. Acquired brain injury and traumatic brain injury are far more common among trauma survivors than the general population knows, and the vast majority of cases are undiagnosed.

The Canadian data is sobering. One in three survivors of brain injury in Canada is a woman who sustained her injury through domestic violence. Most of these injuries were never medically assessed. Most of these women were never told that the forgetfulness, the headaches, the irritability, and the exhaustion they have been living with might not be character flaws or stress. They might be the lingering effects of the strangulation, the shaking, the hitting, or the thrown object that was never brought to a hospital.

One in five men who sustain a brain injury in Canada does so through violence as well. Whether from assault, street violence, sports, or incidents they have never spoken about, many men are also walking around with injuries that have never been named as injuries.

All of this is deeply underreported. Most injuries from violence never reach a clinic. Even when they do, the connection between the violence and the later symptoms is rarely drawn. Nervous system impact layers on top of brain impact in ways that are almost impossible to disentangle without specific expertise. What this means for us as witnesses is simple. Some of the patterns you will encounter across your career, patterns you might read as resistance, distractibility, cognitive decline, emotional volatility, or lack of follow-through, are actually brain injury presenting itself. The body is telling you something. We have not been trained to listen for it.

How Brain Injury Can Show Up in the Room

- Trouble tracking a conversation. The person loses the thread, asks you to repeat yourself, answers a question you did not ask.
- Memory gaps, especially short-term memory. They cannot recall what was said ten minutes ago. They cannot remember whether they have already told you something.
- Difficulty with word-finding. They reach for a word and it is not there.
- Executive function challenges. Trouble planning, organizing, or initiating tasks. Missed appointments. Chronic lateness that has nothing to do with disrespect.
- Severe, often invisible, fatigue. The fatigue does not improve with sleep. It is not the same thing as being tired.
- Sensory overwhelm. Bright lights, loud rooms, crowded spaces, strong scents, even the soft hum of a fan can become intolerable.
- Emotional regulation difficulties. Mood swings that confuse the person more than they confuse you. Tears that come out of nowhere. Irritability that does not match the moment.

- Slower processing. They need more time to respond. Silence after your sentence is often not resistance. It is a brain working through what you said.
- Balance, dizziness, or low-grade nausea.
- Headaches that persist.
- Sleep disruption that does not respond to sleep hygiene.

What the Witness Does With This Knowledge

- Slow down. Speak in shorter sentences. Let there be space between exchanges.
- Do not overload the session. One topic at a time. One task at a time. Breaks written into the structure.
- Offer external supports. A written summary at the end. A voice note they can revisit. Permission to record the session for themselves.
- Do not interpret a scattered presentation as lack of commitment or lack of care. Their body may be doing harder work than yours can see.
- Dim the lights if you can. Soften the sound. Remove strong scents. A low-stimulation room is a kindness, not an accommodation.
- Gently ask, when the relationship can hold it, whether they have ever been medically assessed for brain injury. Many survivors have not. A trauma-informed assessment can change their entire self-understanding. Your question is sometimes the beginning of that possibility.
- Remember that brain injury and nervous system trauma almost always layer. You are not looking for one answer. You are looking for the conditions in which their whole system can settle.

When we fail to see brain injury inside the trauma story, we continue a long tradition of calling survivors difficult, non-compliant, or resistant when their bodies were changed by violence in ways the culture has not learned to read.

Naming brain injury out loud is part of naming the full cost of what was done. It is part of refusing to let the harm keep going unseen. It is also part of leading the world toward the more compassionate care models that survivors have always needed and rarely received.

Children, Teens, and Trauma in Young Bodies

You will sometimes work with young people directly. You will also support parents, grandparents, aunts, uncles, teachers, and coaches who are holding young people through trauma. This section is for both.

What trauma looks like in a child or teen body:

- Behaviour changes. Sudden regressions (bedwetting, clinginess). Sudden rebellions. Sudden withdrawals.
- Somatic complaints without clear medical cause. Stomachaches. Headaches. Sleep disturbances.
- School performance changes in either direction.
- Fear of specific places, people, or situations that did not previously cause fear.
- Changes in eating or sleeping.
- Loss of interest in previously loved activities.

What the adult witness does differently with a young person:

- Match their developmental level. A four-year-old does not need a trauma framework. They need a calm adult who says you are safe and who stays steady.
- Do not interrogate. Children often cannot articulate what happened or may carry shame about it. Gentle presence creates room for the body to tell when it is ready.

- Believe them. Most young people who disclose abuse are telling the truth. The statistics on false reports are very low. The statistics on dismissed true reports are high.
- Involve professionals early. Finding a trauma-informed child therapist, school counsellor, or pediatrician can change a young person's trajectory in ways the everyday witness cannot manage alone.
- For teens specifically, respect their sovereignty over their own story. A teen whose disclosure is immediately broadcast to the whole family may never disclose again.
- Play, art, and movement are often the first languages a young person uses to process trauma. Create space for them without requiring words.

Elders Who Are Finally Speaking

Many elders are now telling stories they have carried for seventy or eighty years. Adult children are becoming the witnesses their parents never had. A grandmother finally speaks about her childhood in the war. A grandfather tells the story of the family secret he has never told anyone. A mother, now in her seventies, names something a sibling did to her in a house that no longer exists.

- The elder's body may not have long. They may be speaking now because they feel time differently.
- The grief they have been carrying has shaped every year of their adult life. Receiving the story now reshapes their final chapter. This is a kind of healing even if it comes late.
- The cognitive resources of an elder may be different from what they were at forty. Follow their pace. Let the story come the way it wants to come.
- You may feel grief for all the years they carried this alone. Let that grief move through you. Do not let it distract from your witnessing.

- If the elder has dementia or cognitive decline, receive fragments as the whole offering they are. A fragment is not a lesser story. It is the story the body can offer today.

Religious and Spiritual Trauma

Religious trauma is a growing and named field. It includes the trauma of high-control religious environments, spiritual abuse by leaders, purity culture, the pressure to believe what the body does not, and the loss of community that often accompanies leaving.

- Leaving a high-control religious environment is often a grief event, not a liberation event, at least at first. The person leaves a whole community, a whole framework, often a whole family.
- Purity culture leaves a specific somatic signature, especially for women and queer people raised inside it. Bodily shame, sexual anxiety, relational difficulty.
- Spiritual abuse, the misuse of religious authority to control, shame, or harm, is a real form of harm. Survivors often carry guilt about feeling harmed by what they were taught was sacred.
- For those who remain inside their tradition while healing, the path is often complex and requires delicate witnessing. Do not pathologize the tradition itself.

Chronic Illness, Disability, and Medical Trauma

Trauma and chronic illness are bidirectional. Chronic stress raises illness risk, and chronic illness itself is trauma-producing. Long COVID, autoimmune conditions, cancer, chronic pain, and other conditions carry weight the medical system routinely dismisses.

Medical trauma is its own category: birth trauma, medical gaslighting, medical racism, dismissive care, invasive procedures without consent, the trauma of being a body whose symptoms are treated as in your head for years before being taken seriously.

- Chronic illness is not a personality trait. Your client is not lazy, dramatic, or attention-seeking. Their body is working hard to function under conditions most bodies would collapse under.
- Flare-ups are not predictable. A client who cancels is not rejecting you.
- The medical system is exhausting. Every interaction takes nervous system resources.
- Medical racism, medical misogyny, and medical dismissiveness of fat, queer, and disabled bodies are well-documented. Your client may have fought years to be taken seriously.
- Disability justice, as a movement, teaches interdependence as a strength. Your client may be your teacher in this.

Climate Grief and Collective Trauma

A generation of clients is coming up with a grief previous generations did not carry. The slow unravelling of a biosphere. The fires. The floods. The species disappearing. The sense that the inheritance is being spent and there will be less to give forward.

- This grief is not irrational. It is a reasonable response to a real crisis.
- Do not try to argue someone out of climate grief with facts about progress. That is not what they need.
- Collective grief rituals offer containers for grief that is too big for an individual to hold alone.
- Climate grief often accompanies a call to meaningful action. Action is part of the healing, not a distraction from it.
- Young clients in particular may need their climate grief acknowledged by the adults around them before they can ever move on to hope.

Digital-Era Trauma

Clients today are embedded in a nervous system context unlike any generation before them. Doomscrolling. Algorithmic rage amplification. AI-mediated relationships. Sextortion, a fast-growing form of abuse particularly targeting young men. Online harassment. The collapse of shared reality.

- Digital harm is real harm. Online bullying is not less damaging than in-person bullying. It may be more, because it follows the person home.
- Sextortion is a documented and rising pattern and has been linked to suicide deaths. A young person who has been sextorted is in acute danger and needs immediate, non-judgmental support and professional help.
- AI-mediated relationships are already part of many clients' lives. They are neither inherently healing nor inherently harmful. They require literacy.
- The algorithmic amplification of rage and despair is a documented effect. A client who seems more angry, more anxious, more hopeless after screen time is having a nervous system response to the design of the platform.

A Pause Before We Build

You have just read through a chapter full of peoples lived realities that may or may not be like your own, patterns, and the specific textures of many different bodies and histories. That chapter is long because the human story is long. You did not read it to become an expert on every community. You read it to widen.

Now the book is about to shift. The next chapter begins the practical craft of building the container. Before it does, sit still for a moment. The rest of this work lives or dies on whether you can answer the question underneath it.

Who are you actually sitting with?

Not in theory. Not in some future practice you have not started. Right now, this week, this season. Who are the humans who come to you? Picture them. Let your body remember them. The friend who texts when she cannot sleep. The colleague who shows up at your desk with a face that means she needs five minutes. The brother who has been quieter on the phone lately. The elder in your community who is starting to want to tell you things. The young person in your program who has stopped making eye contact. The client. The member. The partner. The child.

Write them down. Name them in a notebook you keep nearby. You do not have to show anyone. The naming is private. The naming is how the rest of this book becomes yours.

Then, for each one, ask yourself a small set of questions. Go slowly. There is no right answer. There is only your own answer, honestly met.

What is this person carrying that I know about?

What might they be carrying that I do not know about?

What is their nervous system likely to do when something hard rises?

What do I know about their culture, their history, their lineage, their way of making meaning? What do I still need to learn?

What shape of container would this specific human be able to rest inside?

The work of the chapters ahead is the work of building that container. The container for her, for him, for them.

PART FOUR

The Room

• • •

This is where the work actually happens.

The room can be a living room, a yoga studio, a circle, a boardroom, a hospital corridor, a car ride, a phone call at two in the morning. The room is wherever the holding occurs. Whatever the shape of your room, these chapters walk you through the whole arc. How to build the container. How to hold consent and honour the right to leave. How to know your scope. How to read a nervous system in real time. How to hold a disclosure when it arrives, intact and trembling. How to move a session from its opening to its close without losing the person along the way.

Every sentence here is something you will use. Every practice lives in the body you bring to the room.

CHAPTER TEN

Building the Container: Safety Before Everything

A **container** is the **felt sense** of safety, predictability, and care that holds a space together. It is both structural and relational. It is built before anyone shares a single vulnerable word.

What Makes a Space Feel Safe

Physical safety elements include the actual environment: lighting that does not feel clinical or harsh, seating that allows people to choose their proximity, access to water and the bathroom, and clarity about the duration of the session.

Relational safety elements include how you speak, how you listen, the absence of judgment in your face and your words, and the presence of predictability. Trauma happens in unpredictability. Safety is built through consistency. Mean what you say. Do what you said you would do. Every time.

One-on-One Containers

In a one-on-one space, the container is built primarily through your relationship and your presence. The nervous system of the person across from you is reading you constantly, gathering data about whether you are safe. Your eye contact, your body language, your tone of voice, and your willingness to slow down are all part of what their system registers before their conscious mind does.

- A clear agreement about what this relationship is and what it is not
- Explicit permission to slow down, pause, or redirect at any time

- Clarity about how the person can contact you between sessions
- A shared understanding of how sessions begin and end
- A named process for what happens if the person is in crisis

Group Containers

In a group, every person brings their nervous system into the room, and those systems are in constant, often unconscious communication with each other. One person's **activation** can cascade through a group without a word being spoken.

- **Safer space** agreements co-created with the group, not imposed on them
- Clear norms around confidentiality
- An explicit invitation to participate at one's own level, always
- A named process for how the group will care for someone who becomes distressed
- Regular check-ins throughout the process, not just at the beginning

Co-Creating Safer Space Agreements

There is a difference between a practitioner announcing the rules of the room and a group building the container together. The first is top-down. The second is generative. The second creates ownership. It creates investment. It creates accountability that runs through every nervous system in the circle because people contributed to the very agreements, they are now being asked to honour.

When people co-create safer space agreements, something shifts in the room. They are no longer sitting in a container that someone else built. They are sitting in a container they helped build. Their consciousness of their own responsibility changes. Their awareness of what they can expect from others sharpens. Their nervous system recognizes that they have agency here, that their voice matters, that this space is being shaped by the collective rather than dictated from above.

This is particularly important in trauma-informed work. Many people coming into healing spaces have experienced hierarchical power dynamics that did not serve them. Authoritarian structures. Spaces where their voice did not matter. When we shift to co-creation, we are offering a different experience of power. We are saying: your input matters. Your concerns matter. You are responsible for the health of this container because you helped build it.

Why Safer and Not Safe

Before moving into process, let us anchor why we say "safer space" instead of "safe space." This is important language. No space is truly safe for everyone, all the time. We cannot guarantee that nothing will trigger anyone. Healing work activates things. That is the nature of the work.

What we can do is commit to building a space that is as safe as it can possibly be given the complexity of being human. We can commit to showing up with consciousness. To responding with care. To **repair**ing when harm occurs. To keeping the agreements, we make. We can create conditions where people are more likely to feel held and witnessed and respected. That is safer. That is honest. That is real.

The Process: Seeding, Contributing, Claiming Ownership

The facilitator begins by seeding a few agreements. These are not rules handed down. They are invitations to think together about what the group needs. The facilitator might say: "I want us to build together the agreements that will hold this space for all of us. I am going to name a few places I see us starting, and then I want to hear from you about what else you need."

The facilitator might seed with agreements like these:

Confidentiality: "What is shared here stays here. We honour each other's privacy."

Speaking From I: "When we share, we speak from our own experience. We use 'I' language. We tell our own truth."

Consent Before Advice: "We do not offer unsolicited advice. If you want to share something that has helped you, you ask first."

Right to Pass: "You do not have to participate in anything that does not feel right. You simply say 'I pass.'"

Emotions Welcome Here: "All emotions are welcome. Tears. Anger. Silence. Laughter. Grief. Joy. None need to be fixed."

No Fixing, No Rescuing: "We are here to witness each other. If someone is in a big feeling, we let them be in their process."

Respect Time: "We start on time and end on time. That shows respect for each person's nervous system."

After seeding, the facilitator opens to the group: "*What else does this circle need to function? What agreements would help you feel held here?*"

Each contribution is written down. Each is honoured. The facilitator might gently clarify, but they are not dismissing or editing. This is the group deciding what this container needs.

When people build agreements together, they stop being spectators in their own healing space. They become active agents. They hold agreements they created much more robustly than agreements that were imposed on them.

Facilitation Logistics That Hold the Space

Trauma-informed practice requires more than good intentions. It requires infrastructure. It requires specific logistical choices that tell the nervous system: you are held. You are safe to let your guard down. We have thought about you. We have prepared.

The Hand Gesture Protocol

In group work, you need a nonverbal way for someone to communicate that they are stepping out with intention. When someone leaves without any signal, the group's nervous system often activates. This **ruptures** the container.

Before the circle begins, introduce it: "If you need to step out at any point, simply place your hand on your heart and make eye contact with me. That lets me know you are stepping out with intention and the circle can continue. If someone steps out without that gesture, I will gently check on them. That is love."

If someone does leave without the gesture, the co-facilitator can step out quietly and check in. "Hey, I noticed you stepped out. Are you okay? Do you need anything?"

Virtual Protocols

So much of this work happens on screens now. And while the principles of trauma-informed facilitation are the same whether you are in a room together or separated by thousands of kilometres, the application is significantly different.

Virtual facilitation requires its own set of skills, its own **attunement**, and its own **container**-building practice. It is a different form of in-person work, with its own possibilities and its own particular demands. The screen is a container the body also reads.

Building the Container Digitally

The container does not begin when the call starts. It begins with every communication that precedes it: the invitation, the confirmation, the instructions for joining. Each of these touchpoints is an opportunity to build the **felt sense** of safety before the screen opens.

- Send a warm, clear welcome message before the session that orients the person to what to expect
- Include simple technical guidance so they are not arriving anxious about the technology
- Suggest they find a private, physically comfortable space where they will not be interrupted
- Recommend they have water nearby and, if possible, their feet on the floor
- Name that stepping away from the camera at any time is completely acceptable

Reading Nervous System Signals Through a Screen

On video, you lose access to the lower half of the body entirely, and much of the nuance of the upper body. This means your attunement must become more refined in the channels that are still available to you.

What to Watch for on Video

- Eye contact changes: looking away from the camera frequently, eyes going fixed or glassy, increased blinking
- Facial colour changes: flushing or pallor visible even on screen
- Breath: visible in the shoulders and chest, you can often see breath become shallower
- Jaw and mouth tension
- The quality of stillness: a frozen quality that feels different from ease
- Sudden subject changes or redirection
- Audio changes: voice flattening, speeding up, going quiet

- The person moving physically away from the camera, even slightly
- Looking off screen repeatedly as a sign of **activation**
- Appearing to go through the motions while something is shut down underneath

The Challenge of the Freeze Response on Video

One of the most important distinctions to make in virtual facilitation: a person who has frozen or dissociated can look almost identical to a person experiencing a poor internet connection. Both may become still. Both may have a glassy quality. Both may fail to respond immediately.

If you notice this quality and are uncertain, name it gently and warmly. 'I notice you have gone a little quiet. I want to check in with you. How are you doing right now?' This serves both possibilities. If it is technical, the question prompts them to reconnect. If it is nervous system, the question brings them back into relationship.

Managing Technical Difficulties with Trauma-Informed Awareness

Technical difficulties in a virtual session are not just inconvenient. For a person who is in a vulnerable state or who has difficulty with unpredictability, a dropped connection, a frozen screen, or audio failure can be genuinely activating.

- Name at the start of every virtual session that technology can be unpredictable, and state what you will do if the connection breaks: 'If we get disconnected, I will send you a message within two minutes and we will reconnect.'
- Practise genuine equanimity with technical issues. Your calm in that moment is the message.

- When reconnecting after a disruption, acknowledge it. 'That was a little disorienting. How are you doing? Are you still with me?'
- Do not rush to pick up where you left off. Re-establish connection first.

The Chat Function as a Gentler Entry Point

In virtual group facilitation, the chat function is one of the most powerful trauma-informed tools you have. For a person who is not ready to speak, who needs more time to process before responding verbally, or who experiences group speaking as activating, the chat offers a lower-stakes way to participate.

- Name the chat as a valid form of participation at the start of every session
- Respond to chat contributions with the same warmth you would give a spoken response
- Offer chat-based check-ins: 'If you would like to share where you are landing, feel free to drop a word or an emoji in the chat. There is no pressure to.'
- Consider offering private chat as an option for people to reach you during the session without speaking aloud

Your Own Presence on Screen

What you project through a screen is amplified in some ways and reduced in others. Your voice and your face carry more weight virtually than they might in person, because they are the primary channels available.

- Ensure your lighting is on your face, not behind you. Being backlit makes you appear as a silhouette and reduces the warmth of your presence significantly.
- Position your camera at eye level so you are making genuine eye contact with the person, not looking down at them or up at them

- Slow your speech slightly. The compression of audio on most platforms means nuance is lost at speed.
- Pause longer than you think you need to. Lag is real, and a person who is working up the courage to speak needs those extra seconds.
- Your background matters. A chaotic or impersonal background communicates something. A simple, warm, intentional space communicates that you prepared for them.

Distance does not diminish the capacity for genuine presence. Presence is not about proximity. It is about attention. And attention is something you can offer through any medium when you have learned to give it fully.

The Co-Facilitator or Support Role

If you are doing group work in person or virtually and you want to be trauma-informed, you need at least one other person in the room. Their role is vital and distinct.

The co-facilitator is the second set of eyes on the room. They notice if someone is shutting down. They notice if someone's process is becoming so large that it is consuming the group's energy.

Never run group work in a trauma-informed way alone. Your own nervous system will become dysregulated trying to hold everything. Having a co-facilitator is not a luxury. It is a necessary part of trauma-informed facilitation.

Diplomacy in Sharing: Consent Before Advice

One of the most damaging things that can happen in a healing space is unsolicited advice. Someone shares something tender, and another person immediately jumps in with solutions. This is a form of boundary crossing.

In a trauma-informed group, we practice consent before sharing any advice. The agreement is: "If you want to offer a suggestion, you ask first. 'Would it be helpful if I shared something that worked for me?' And you wait for the answer."

This practice is about creating a culture where people move through the world with more consciousness about the impact of their words and actions. It starts in the circle.

Long-Term Group Dynamics

When a group meets over time, a relational ecosystem develops. Patterns emerge. Old wounds are re-enacted within the group itself. Power dynamics surface. Attachment patterns become visible. People begin to experience the group the way they experienced their family of origin.

In long-term group work, the container must be tended, not just set. This means revisiting agreements when the group shifts, naming dynamics as they arise without shaming anyone, and holding space for ruptures and genuine repair.

Rupture and Repair

In any facilitated relationship, moments of rupture will happen. What matters is repair. Repair is the practice of acknowledging what happened, naming its impact, and working together to restore connection. For people who grew up in environments where repair was never modelled, experiencing genuine repair in your facilitated space can be profoundly healing in itself.

What Rupture Looks Like in Practice

Rupture in a facilitated space can look many different ways. In person, it might look like a participant expressing frustration with an activity, becoming visibly agitated during a discussion, withdrawing completely after feeling unheard, or challenging the facilitator's authority in front of the group. It might look like two participants having a tense exchange. It might look like silence that carries something unspoken and heavy.

In virtual spaces, rupture is often quieter but equally real. A participant turns off their camera and does not return. Someone sends a sharp message in the chat. A person who was engaged goes silent. Someone logs off without warning. The energy in the virtual room shifts, and you can feel the collective nervous system tighten.

Between sessions, rupture might surface as an email expressing hurt, a complaint to an organizer, or a participant who simply stops showing up.

All of these are information. All of these deserve attention.

The Practice of Repair

Repair is the practice of acknowledging that something happened, naming it with honesty, and tending to it with care. Repair does not mean fixing. It does not mean the discomfort goes away. It means the relationship, the container, the trust is attended to rather than ignored.

Repair in person might sound like this:

- "I want to name something I noticed in our last session. There was a moment where the energy in the room shifted, and I want to check in about that. How did that land for you?"
- "I am aware that what I said may not have landed the way I intended. I want to take responsibility for that and hear how it affected you."
- "I noticed you stepped back from the group after that exchange. I want you to know I saw that, and I care about how you are doing."
- Repair in virtual spaces might sound like this:
- "I noticed your camera went off during our session yesterday. I wanted to reach out privately and check in. How are you?"

- "I am sending this message because I want to make sure you felt held in our last call. If anything did not sit right, I want to hear that."
- "Something felt unresolved when we ended our last session. I would love to take a few minutes at the start of our next one to tend to that."

The key elements of repair are: timeliness (do not let ruptures sit unaddressed), accountability (own your part without defensiveness), curiosity (ask rather than assume), and care (the person matters more than the agenda).

Repair is itself a healing act. For many people, rupture without repair is the pattern they know. Arguments that were never resolved. Harm that was never acknowledged. Pain that was never tended to. When you model repair, when you show that relationships can withstand rupture and come back stronger, you are offering something profoundly reparative.

Setting Tone from the Very First Moment

The container begins before the formal beginning. It begins when someone reads your intake form, receives your welcome message, or first steps into your space.

- The warmth and clarity of your written communications
- How you greet someone when they arrive, verbally and physically
- Whether your opening includes an invitation to arrive in the body: a breath, a moment of landing
- Your willingness to acknowledge that being in this space takes courage

Rupture and Repair: Relationality Is the Work

Every framework in this book, every practice, every grounding tool, every map of the nervous system, is scaffolding. The scaffolding is important. It holds the shape while the real thing takes place. The real thing is relational. The real thing is what happens in the live connection between your nervous system and the nervous system of the person you are with. Relationality is not the setting for the work. Relationality is the work.

This matters because trauma is almost always relational. Most of the pain a human brings to a witnessing space was received in connection with another human. The absent parent. The caregiver who could not stay regulated. The partner who used closeness as a weapon. The community that withdrew when the truth was spoken. The institution that turned away. Where the wound lives, the healing must also live. The body cannot metabolize relational pain in isolation. It needs another body. It needs another regulated, present, staying body.

You are that body. The work you do is not something you give from the outside. It is the quality of relationship itself.

Rupture Is Not Failure. Rupture Is the Practice.

Attachment researchers like Beatrice Beebe and Edward Tronick have shown something that should change how we carry our own inevitable mistakes. Even in the most securely attached infant caregiver pairs, there is misattunement happening roughly one third of the time. The securely attached infant is not one whose caregiver was perfect. The securely attached infant is one whose caregiver repaired.

Rupture is the ordinary texture of being in relationship. You will miss a cue. You will say the wrong thing. You will lose presence for a moment and the person across from you will feel it. You will forget something they told you. You will be tired and short and inaccessible on a Tuesday when they needed you to be the steady one. None of this is failure. All of this is the predictable weather of two nervous systems in contact.

What determines whether the witnessing space is safe enough to do deep work is not whether rupture happens. Rupture always happens.

What determines safety is whether repair is available. Repair is the decisive practice.

What Repair Actually Looks Like

Repair is small. Repair is specific. Repair is almost always delivered in a quieter voice than the rupture.

Repair sounds like: I missed what you just said. Can you say it again? I can see I reached for advice when you needed me to stay. I am sorry. Let me slow down. Something shifted in you a moment ago and I moved too fast. I want to come back to that. I got defensive when you named that, and that was mine, not yours. I lost you for a second. I am here.

Repair does not include a long defence of your intent. Repair does not include making the person who was hurt comfort you. Repair does not include a speech about how hard you are trying. Repair is the acknowledgment, the ownership, the return. Then silence. Then whatever they need next.

For many of the humans who will sit with you, consistent repair is something they have never experienced. Repair in their family of origin might have been denial, gaslighting, performance of apology with nothing changing, or a shift in the relationship that made them feel guilty for having felt the rupture in the first place. Your willingness to repair cleanly teaches their body something their history may have never taught it. That staying is possible after mistake. That closeness survives honesty. That the relationship is bigger than the moment that just hurt.

When Repair Happens, a New Story Becomes Possible

A body that has survived by expecting abandonment, betrayal, or collapse after every vulnerable moment does not take a single repair and rewrite its internal story. But it takes note. And the next repair takes note. And the one after that takes note. Over time, the body begins to hold a new possibility quietly alongside the old protective one. The new possibility is that some relationships do not end when something hard is felt. Some people come back.

This is slow work. You will not see it happen in a single session. You will see it in a text six months in that says something you could not have imagined receiving at the beginning. You will see it when someone who used to leave the room at the first hint of conflict begins to stay. You will see it in the way their shoulders drop when they walk into your space. Their body is rewriting.

The medicine is not what you do for them. The medicine is who you are able to stay as, in relationship, through rupture and back to repair.

When you accept that relationality is the work itself, you can stop reaching for the perfect intervention. There is no perfect intervention. There is only the next moment of presence, the next breath, the next honest return. That is the whole practice. Everything else is scaffolding.

How Groups Become Containers:

There are many ways this book supports the work, from a one-on-one witnessing space. A friend and a friend. A practitioner and a client. A leader and a member of their team. There's this one-on-one and there are groups. Workshops. Circles. Ceremonies. Support groups. Classrooms. Teams of people who gather for something hard. Holding a group is not a scaled-up version of holding one person. Holding a group is its own discipline, with its own phases, its own kind of staying.

In 1965, a researcher named Bruce Tuckman proposed a model for how groups move. He later added a fifth phase. The five phases are

Forming, Storming, Norming, Performing, and Adjourning. The model is usually taught in business schools. It is almost never taught to healers, facilitators, elders, or community holders. That is a loss. Every group you will ever hold moves through these phases whether you name them or not. How you hold the group through each phase is a huge part of the role of a sacred witness.

The phases are not clinical theory. They are a map of the relational weather a room of nervous systems will predictably pass through together. Knowing the map changes what you can hold.

Forming: The Nervous Systems Are Introducing Themselves

In the first moments of a group, every body in the room is scanning. Eyes are checking exits. Breath is shallow. People are performing a version of themselves that is acceptable enough to be in the space. This is protection. No nervous system drops its guard on instinct alone.

Your job in forming is to create the soft landing. Before content, before curriculum, before teaching, the container has to be named and shown. Where are the bathrooms? What time will we end? What do I ask of you and what do I not ask of you? What language do we use here? Who is in the room and how do we want to be together? Your calm, your slowness, your willingness to name the ordinary is what begins to convince bodies that this space is worth softening into.

Do not rush forming. Five minutes of real arrival is worth more than an hour of content people cannot receive because their nervous system never landed.

Storming: The Bodies Test the Container

If you hold the group long enough, storming comes. It almost always does. Someone questions you. Someone arrives late and with an edge. Someone challenges the premise of the work. Two people in the room have a tension that becomes audible. Someone cries and you can feel the rest of the group tighten. Someone leaves the room and nobody knows whether they are coming back.

This is the group checking whether the container is real. A body that has lived through unreliable containers will test. It will push. It will see if the holder can stay. If the holder flinches, shames the tester, withdraws, or abandons the container, everybody in the room receives the information that this is another space like the ones that broke them before.

Your job in storming is to stay. Breathe. Slow your voice. Hold the container without becoming rigid. Name what you see without making anyone wrong. Something hard just happened. I want us to stay with it. A body that sees you stay through a storm begins to trust the container in a way that words alone cannot teach.

Storming is the cost of admission to the deeper work. If you try to skip it, you will never reach performing. Storming is not a bug. It is a feature.

Norming: Something Settles

After storming, if the container has held, something settles. The room softens. Laughter shows up where there was none. People begin to speak more honestly. Side conversations become supportive rather than protective. A culture begins to emerge that belongs to this particular group in this particular season. The group is becoming itself.

Your job in norming is to protect what is emerging. Do not rush it. Do not over-teach. Witness the settling. Notice the new trust. Let the group feel itself becoming a group. Your role shifts from holder of individual safety to holder of the collective field.

Performing: The Real Work Begins

When a group is performing, the depth is possible. Disclosures arrive that nobody could have spoken in week one. Somatic shifts happen.

Body-level healing becomes available because the nervous system has been trained by the group itself that this is a place that can hold it. Members do work for each other that you cannot do. Something alive and collective is in the room.

Your job in performing is to be the calm. Hold steady. Do not need anything from the group. Do not need applause or breakthrough or movement. Witness what is. Trust the group to do its own medicine. This is the phase where the group does not need you less. It needs you differently. It needs you to be the quiet bedrock while the life happens on top of you.

Adjourning: Closing With Care

Every group ends. The last session of the workshop. The final ceremony. The graduation of the cohort. The moment the circle stops meeting. Groups that do not close consciously leave unresolved nervous system tension in every body that was part of them. Members walk away with a subtle unfinished ache they may not be able to name.

Your job in adjourning is to close with ceremony. Name what happened. Name what was built. Let each person speak if they want to. Let grief be in the room, because ending always involves grief, even when the group is also ready to end. Mark the transition in some embodied way. A breath together. A circle. A ritual. A moment of shared silence. The body remembers endings. Help this one be the kind of ending that nourishes.

The way a group closes teaches its members something about how endings can happen. For someone whose life has held many unmetabolized endings, a conscious adjourning can itself be medicine.

Holding the Group Is the Sacred Witness Role

Every phase asks something different of you. Forming asks for warmth and clarity. Storming asks for nervous system steadiness under pressure. Norming asks for patience and protection of what is still soft.

Performing asks for a kind of quiet you can only produce when your own self-care is sound. Adjourning asks for ceremony and willingness to grieve alongside the group.

How you hold the group is the work. The curriculum matters less than you think. The worksheets matter less than you think. The clever exercises matter less than you think. The felt safety of the container, across all five phases, is what lets real change occur in the bodies gathered in front of you. Your steadiness is the curriculum.

Hold the group the way you would hold a precious thing. Because you are.

CHAPTER ELEVEN

Consent, Autonomy, and the Right to Leave

Consent is not a form you sign at the beginning of a session. It is a living practice that breathes through every moment of the work.

For many of the people you will work with, their history includes having their choices taken from them. Their bodies. Their voices. Their ability to say no. When you practice genuine, ongoing consent, you are offering a direct counter-experience to one of the most fundamental wounds trauma creates: the loss of sovereignty.

Why Coercion Is Triggering

Coercion, even subtle and well-intentioned coercion, is one of the fastest routes to nervous system **activation** for a trauma survivor. This is because the nervous system does not evaluate the content of a pressure; it evaluates the feeling of being unable to choose freely. And that feeling, the sense of being pushed, of having no real option, replicates exactly what happened in the original wounding.

What Coercion Looks Like

- Saying 'I really think it would help you to share' after someone has already declined
- Using positive group energy to pressure participation
- Repeating an invitation multiple times after a no, however gently
- Framing withdrawal as avoidance or resistance rather than wisdom
- Responding to someone's no with visible disappointment, however briefly

- Implying that healing requires engagement with the specific activity you have designed

What Non-Coercive Practice Sounds Like

- 'I am going to invite you to try this. There is no should here. If it does not feel right for you today, simply being present is more than enough.'
- 'You are welcome to step out, close your eyes, or simply observe. All of those are valid forms of participation.'
- 'If at any point you want to pause or stop, you can simply place your hand on your chest and I will know to give you space.'
- After a no: 'Thank you for knowing that about yourself.' And then moving forward without returning to the invitation.

Consent Throughout, During, and After

Consent is renewed with each new invitation, each transition, each moment of potential vulnerability. Check in when you notice a shift. 'I want to pause for a moment. Are you still with me? How is this landing?' This kind of checking is not a performance of care. It is care itself.

The Right to Withdraw With Honour and Dignity

Every person you work with has the absolute right to withdraw from any part of the process at any time, including the whole relationship, without having to justify it, explain themselves, or endure any consequence to how they are treated.

How to Name the Right to Withdraw

Before any engagement, say something like:

'You always have the right to slow down, pause, step back from any part of this, or end our work together entirely. That is sovereignty over your own healing journey, and I will always honour it.'

CHAPTER TWELVE

Knowing Your Scope: When to Refer

There is no braver act in a healing space than saying: this is beyond what I can safely hold, and I know where to find someone who can.

Signs That You May Be Out of Your Scope

- The person is expressing active suicidality or self-harm
- You are hearing trauma disclosures that are leaving you activated and unable to regulate
- The person is showing signs of psychosis or a break from shared reality
- Substance use or a mental health condition is significantly impacting their ability to engage
- The cultural context of their pain is so far outside your experience that you cannot accompany it without risk of harm
- The weight of the work is significantly impacting your own mental health
- You feel a pull to rescue rather than witness

Scope Assessment: A Yes/No Reflection Tool

This is a tool for honest self-reflection. It is designed to help you discern whether you are the right support for the person in front of you, right now, given what they are carrying and what you are carrying alongside them.

There is no score. There is no pass or fail. A single *yes* in the right place is enough to warrant a pause, a conversation with a supervisor or peer, or a referral. Knowing your scope is one of the most sacred acts of care you can offer.

Complete this before, during, or after working with someone who is activating something in you. Return to it as often as you need.

The Person in Front of You

	Yes	No
1. Is this person expressing thoughts of suicide, self-harm, or harm to others?	□	□
2. Is this person describing symptoms that sound like psychosis, a break from shared reality, or severe dissociation that does not resolve with grounding?	□	□
3. Is substance use or a mental health condition significantly impacting their ability to engage in the work?	□	□
4. Are the trauma disclosures you are receiving leaving you activated, unable to regulate, or emotionally flooded session after session?	□	□
5. Is the cultural context of this person's pain so far outside your lived experience that you cannot accompany it without risk of causing harm?	□	□
6. Does this person need medical, psychiatric, or clinical support that you are not trained or licensed to provide?	□	□

Your Own Capacity Right Now

	Yes	No
7. Is the weight of this work significantly impacting your own mental health, sleep, or daily functioning?	□	□
8. Do you feel a pull to rescue this person rather than witness them?	□	□
9. Are you avoiding certain topics or sessions because of what this person might bring?	□	□
10. Have you lost your ability to remain regulated in their presence?	□	□
11. Are you carrying this person's story outside of session in a way that feels consuming rather than professional?	□	□
12. Do you find yourself offering reassurance rather than presence, because their pain activates your own?	□	□

The Relational Field Between You

	Yes	No
13. Has the therapeutic or facilitative relationship become one where the person is dependent on you in a way that exceeds your role?	□	□
14. Are you holding dual roles with this person (friend, family member, colleague, community member) in a way that compromises your ability to serve them clearly?	□	□
15. Has trust been ruptured in a way you do not have the tools or support to repair?	□	□

A Moment of Honest Reflection

If you answered *yes* to even one of these questions, pause here. Breathe. That honesty is the work.

Referring someone is an act of deep care. It means you are prioritizing their healing over your comfort, your ego, or your desire to be the one who holds it all. The most trauma-informed thing you will ever do is say: *I love you enough to hand you to someone who can meet you where I cannot.*

You are not failing. You are honouring the boundary that keeps both of you safe.

How to Refer Without Stigma

'I have been thinking about what would most support you right now, and I believe you deserve to also have someone in your corner who specializes specifically in this area. This is me making sure you have everything you need. Staying close and bringing in specialized support are both part of holding you well. Would it be okay if I shared a contact I trust?"

The Adverse Childhood Experiences (ACE) Study, conducted by the Centers for Disease Control and Prevention (CDC) in partnership with Kaiser Permanente and first published in 1998, remains one of the largest investigations into the relationship between childhood adversity and long-term health outcomes. What it revealed was staggering in its clarity: nearly two-thirds of participants reported at least one adverse childhood experience. More than one in five reported three or more. Globally, the World Health Organization estimates that up to one billion children experience violence or neglect each year. This is the human condition, unmasked. What this tells us, as practitioners, is something the body already knows. The people who walk into your space, your circle, your session, are statistically likely to be carrying unprocessed pain. Many of them have survived violence, neglect, household dysfunction, or the slow erosion of growing up in systems that were never designed to hold them. They are the norm. And something is shifting.

As the world becomes more connected, as language around healing becomes more accessible, as communities begin naming what was once unspeakable, more people are turning toward their own inner work. This is an inevitability. When human beings are given even a small opening to understand their own pain, they will walk toward it. They will seek support. They will look for someone to witness them on the journey. This means the demand for healing support will continue to grow. And with it, the responsibility to ensure that the people we connect them to are equipped to hold what arrives.

Here is what matters: there are many skilled, trained clinical professionals doing exceptional, trauma-informed work. Licensed therapists, psychologists, counsellors, social workers, and psychiatrists who understand that a person's responses are intelligent adaptations, not pathologies to be corrected. These practitioners exist, and they are invaluable allies in the healing ecosystem. The distinction worth paying attention to when referring someone to a professional is whether their approach honours the whole person or reduces them to a set of symptoms. A practitioner who pathologizes without context, who diagnoses without curiosity, who treats the label instead of the human, can inadvertently reinforce the very wounds a person is trying to heal. For someone on a self-directed healing journey, this can feel like a door closing just as they found the courage to open it.

When you are connecting someone to clinical support, look for practitioners who demonstrate the following:

They ask about experience before they assign language to it. They are curious about context, culture, and history before reaching for a diagnosis. They speak about responses as adaptations, not deficits. They make space for the body in the conversation: the breath, nervous system, and felt sense of safety. They name their own scope clearly, and they do not shame for seeking support outside of clinical settings. They understand that healing is not linear and do not measure progress against a standardized timeline. They hold autonomy as sacred. They will never position themselves as the authority over anyone's own inner knowing. They welcome collaboration with other practitioners and modalities rather than dismissing what falls outside their training. They are willing to say, "I don't know," and to learn alongside others. They create a container where there's felt safety enough to be honest, and where honesty is met with care rather than correction.

These are not unreasonable expectations. They are the baseline of trauma-informed practice. And the people seeking healing deserve to know what that baseline looks like so they can advocate for themselves inside any clinical relationship.

The world is waking up. The people are coming. Our work is to make sure the path they find leads somewhere safe. There is space for all of us to work together and have integrative approaches, rather than us and them ideas about what it means to care for people on their healing journey. All ways matter.

CHAPTER THIRTEEN

Reading the Nervous System: What the Body Tells You

One of the most important skills a trauma-informed practitioner develops is the ability to read the body. Not to diagnose. Not to analyse. But to witness.

The nervous system communicates constantly through the body, and it does so faster than words. By the time someone tells you they are fine, their body may have already been telling you something entirely different for several minutes.

Signs of Nervous System Activation

Vocal and Relational Indicators

- A sudden flattening or change in tone: the voice becoming monotone or robotic
- Speaking much more quickly or much more slowly than before
- Laughing at something that is not funny, a freeze or **fawn response**
- Excessive agreeing or yes-ing
- Sudden subject changes, redirection, or deflection with humour
- Going quiet in a way that feels different from peaceful quiet
- Over-explaining or rambling as a way to stay in the cognitive mind and out of the body
- Giving short, closed answers when they were expansive before

Each response is an act of intelligence. The nervous system chose it because at some point, it worked. Your role is not to fix the response. Your role is to make the space safe enough that the person can eventually choose differently.

The Difference Between Peaceful and Checked Out

Stillness in a session can be presence. It can also be **dissociation**. The difference is relational. A person who is peacefully present feels available, even in their stillness. A person who has dissociated or frozen may look calm but feels absent. The eyes may have a fixed quality. There is a sense of the light going off behind them.

If you sense someone has left the room in this way, do not push them back through the content. Invite them gently back into the room itself. 'I notice you have gone a little quiet. I am going to slow down. Can you feel your feet on the floor?'

This distinction requires tremendous care in how it is communicated. A person who has dissociated has not chosen to check out. Their nervous system has taken them somewhere protective because the present moment became too much. Calling attention to someone's dissociation in a way that feels accusatory, asking them to pay attention, expressing frustration at their seeming disconnection, is one of the most harmful things a facilitator can do. It replicates the very dynamic that caused the protective response in the first place: being punished for a survival mechanism.

Instead, your invitation back is always gentle, always warm, always optional: "I am going to invite us all to feel our feet on the floor right now. Just notice the ground." You are speaking to the room, which gives the dissociated person an on-ramp back into their body without being singled out.

Buffer Time and Nervous System Recovery

After any content that might be activating, heavy, or emotionally demanding, build in **buffer time**. This is non-negotiable. The nervous system cannot move from **activation** to content absorption without transition. If you move directly from a tender topic into the next agenda item, you are asking people to override their biology. Some will dissociate. Some will shut down. Some will leave.

Buffer time looks like movement: standing, stretching, shaking out the body. It looks like a water break. It looks like a **grounding** practice. It looks like naming what just happened: "We just covered something that may have stirred things up. Let us take a few minutes to land. Move your body if you need to. Drink some water. Breathe." This validates the experience. It tells people: what you are feeling is expected and honoured.

This practice also models that healing work includes rest. That the nervous system needs oscillation: engagement and recovery, depth and surface, intensity and gentleness. This rhythm is how the body metabolizes experience.

Content Disclaimers and the Practice of Informed Choice

Before introducing any content, practice, or topic that might be activating, share a disclaimer. This is a fundamental trauma-informed practice. It is how we honour **autonomy** and informed **consent** in real time.

A **content disclaimer** sounds like: "What we are about to explore touches on themes of grief and loss. I want you to know that before we go in, so you can make a choice about how you want to participate. You can engage fully, you can observe, you can step away. All of those are valid."

For **somatic** practices, it might sound like: "I am going to invite you into a body-based exercise. This involves closing your eyes and noticing physical sensations. If that does not feel safe for you right now, you are welcome to keep your eyes open and simply observe. There is no pressure."

Disclaimers are not about creating fear or over-**pathologizing** the content. They are about giving people the information they need to make a sovereign choice about their own participation. This itself is healing. For many people, being given a genuine choice about what they will be exposed to is something they have rarely experienced.

In virtual spaces, disclaimers can also be shared in writing via the chat, which gives people a private, non-performative way to make their choice.

What to Do When You Notice Activation

- Name what you observe, gently and without alarm: 'I notice we seem to have landed somewhere tender. Let us slow down.'
- Offer a grounding practice: feet on the floor, a breath, a slow look around the room to name five things they can see.
- Offer the choice to pause or redirect without any suggestion that this is a setback.
- If appropriate, sit with them in silence for a moment. Not every activation requires words.
- After stabilization, check in before continuing: 'How are you feeling now? Would you like to continue, or would something else serve you better?'

Recognizing and Responding to Each Trauma Response

Knowing the four stress responses by name is the beginning. Knowing what each one actually looks like when it is sitting across from you in a session, in a real human body, with real texture and nuance, is the skill that changes everything.

Each response has its own signature. Its own quality of presence. Its own set of needs. And each one calls for a different kind of accompaniment from you. What helps a person in freeze can further activate a person in fight. What softens flight can be exactly the wrong move for fawn. This is why broad, one-size facilitation approaches fall short with trauma survivors. The nervous system requires precision. It requires that you can tell the difference.

The Fight Response

What it looks like

The **fight response** is the one most likely to be misread as personality. As attitude. As resistance. As someone being difficult.

In a facilitation space, fight rarely looks like physical aggression. It is far more likely to look like this: the person challenges your framing. They push back on an activity before trying it. They cross their arms, lean back, and meet your words with visible skepticism. Their jaw is set. Their voice has an edge. They ask pointed questions that feel less like curiosity and more like a test. They may be argumentative, dismissive, or quick to point out what is wrong with what you have offered.

Their body is mobilized. You may notice the shoulders squaring, the chest rising, the chin lifting slightly. The eyes are direct, sometimes uncomfortably so. The breath is faster and higher in the chest. The voice may be louder, harder, or clipped. There is energy in the room that has a pressing quality to it, and it is pressing toward you.

In longer interactions you may notice this person consistently arriving on the edge of conflict, looking for the moment the space becomes unsafe, ready to respond to that moment before it arrives. They are not wrong to be ready. Their history taught them to be.

What is happening underneath

Fight is the nervous system's attempt to create safety through power. The message the body is sending is: if I can establish dominance or control in this interaction, I will be safe. This is especially common in people whose early experiences taught them that vulnerability was dangerous, that softness got them hurt, or that the only way to survive was to be the one with more power in the room.

What presents as confrontation is often profound fear. The person fighting you in a session is, underneath that armour, often terrified. The aggression is the traum-our. It is what grew over the wound to protect it.

How to support someone in fight

Stay regulated. This is the first and most essential thing. If their fight response activates yours, the room will escalate. Your calm is not passivity. Your calm is the intervention.

Do not increase your authority in the moment. This seems counterintuitive, but leaning into your facilitator role more firmly when someone is in fight often intensifies their response. Instead, reduce the power differential as much as possible. Come off your platform. Slow down. Soften.

Give them something they can have control over. Offer a genuine choice. The experience of genuine choice can shift the nervous system significantly because control is exactly what the fight response is seeking.

Every person in your space is having a normal response to the life they have lived. Your role is to make that normal response feel safe enough to be felt, seen, and slowly, gently, metabolized.

The Flight Response

What it looks like

Flight in a facilitation space is the response that looks like everything except what it is. It looks like distraction. Busyness. Avoidance. Leaving.

The person in flight is moving, physically or mentally, away from what is activating them. You may see them glancing toward the door or window. Checking their phone. Bringing up unrelated topics. Asking questions that redirect the conversation. Finding reasons to stand up, to get water, to adjust their seat. Arriving late and leaving early.

In the body: the person may be in constant subtle motion. Tapping, fidgeting, bouncing a leg. The eyes move frequently rather than holding steady contact. The energy feels scattered or elusive. You may notice you have trouble **tracking** them, that conversations with them seem to slide away from depth before they arrive there. Every time you move toward something meaningful, there is a redirection.

In groups, the person in flight may be the most socially active. Chatty, charming, engaged on the surface, always present in a room in a way that somehow keeps them from ever having to be still within it. The movement is the protection.

What is happening underneath

Flight is the nervous system's attempt to create safety through distance. The message is: if I can get far enough away from the thing that is threatening me, I will survive it. Underneath flight is often a deep longing to be present. Many people in chronic flight are exhausted by their own movement. They want to land. They have not yet learned that landing is safe.

How to support someone in flight

Create gentler on-ramps into depth. The person in flight will not walk directly into vulnerable territory. They need permission to approach it sideways, at their own pace, without feeling cornered. Offer indirect access: metaphor, creative activities, writing, art, movement.

Match their pace before slowing it. If they are moving fast, meet them there briefly before gradually inviting more stillness. Grounding practices are particularly helpful for flight. The 5-4-3-2-1 sensory orientation works well because it gives the need for movement and scanning something constructive to do.

The Freeze Response

What it looks like

Freeze is the response most likely to go unseen, and it is one of the most important to be able to identify.

The person in freeze may appear, on the surface, to be the easiest person in the room to work with. They are quiet. Compliant. Still. They do not push back. They do not redirect. They do not leave. And yet something is missing. The quality of aliveness that is present in an engaged person is not there. The light has gone somewhere else.

In the body: a quality of stillness that is different from ease. The face may be flat, expressionless, or wearing a mask of pleasantness that does not reach the eyes. The eyes themselves may have a fixed, glassy quality, or may be looking at you without genuinely seeing you. The breath is shallow, barely perceptible. The voice, when it comes, may be monotone, slow, or oddly flat in affect.

You may notice a particular quality in the room when someone is frozen: a slight unreachability. A sense that the words are not quite arriving. That you are speaking into a space where the person used to be.

What is happening underneath

Freeze is the oldest of the stress responses, the one that predates fight and flight in evolutionary history. It is what the body does when neither fighting nor fleeing is possible or safe. It is the system shutting down to protect the organism from the full impact of an overwhelming experience.

Freeze is especially common in people who were harmed in situations where movement was not possible: childhood abuse, medical trauma, sexual violence, situations of captivity or profound powerlessness. When the body learned that stillness was survival, it returns to that response whenever survival feels uncertain.

How to support someone in freeze

Move slowly and without pressure. Any increase in pace, volume, or intensity will deepen the freeze rather than lifting it. Your slow, steady, warm presence is the primary tool.

Do not attempt to process emotional content with someone who is frozen. The **freeze response** means the integrative capacity of the brain is temporarily offline. Moving into therapeutic depth with someone who is not neurologically available for it is unlikely to produce anything useful and may deepen their sense of overwhelm. Wait for the thaw. It will come. Keep the space warm until it does.

Language for the Freeze Response

- 'Can you feel the weight of your body in the seat right now?'
- 'Can you look around the room and find something that catches your eye?'
- 'I notice you might be somewhere far away right now. That is completely okay. I am not going anywhere. Take all the time you need.'
- Warm your tone and slow your speech to the pace of a lullaby. This activates the **parasympathetic nervous system** through the vagal pathways in ways that words alone cannot.
- Do not require verbal response. Let presence be enough.

The Fawn Response

What it looks like

Fawn is the response that requires the most practitioner skill to see. Because from the outside, it looks like the ideal client.

The person who is fawning agrees with everything you say. They complete every activity with apparent enthusiasm. They give you warm feedback at the end of the session. They tell you the workshop was exactly what they needed. They thank you more than the moment seems to call for. They apologize for taking up space even while occupying very little of it.

In the body: the face is arranged in pleasantness, a particular kind of brightness that has a slightly effortful quality if you look closely enough. The body is often oriented toward you, leaning in, attentive, performing engagement. The voice is agreeable, warm, slightly higher than their natural register. They laugh at the right moments. They validate your points before you have finished making them.

What they rarely do is disagree. What they rarely do is say I do not want to do this. The subtler signs: they mirror your language back to you rather than generating their own. Their answers to reflective questions have a quality of telling you what they think you want to hear. They seem to have no strong preferences of their own. They are extraordinarily easy to work with, and that ease is worth paying close attention to.

What is happening underneath

Fawn is the nervous system's attempt to create safety through becoming what the perceived threat wants you to be. It says: if I can make you happy, if I can be agreeable enough, pleasing enough, then I will be safe. The danger will not come.

This response is almost always learned in childhood, in environments where a child's safety depended on the emotional state of someone with power over them. The person who fawns in your space is likely extraordinarily skilled at reading people. And they are using those skills to keep themselves safe from the version of you they are waiting to appear. Real presence is a later arrival, available only once the body has verified that no other version of you is coming.

How to support someone in fawn

Remove your own approval from the equation as explicitly and as often as possible. The fawn response is sustained by the sense that your satisfaction matters to their safety. When you actively communicate that it does not, that there is nothing they can do to lose your care, you begin to loosen that equation.

Celebrate the authentic response over the agreeable one. When someone does express a genuine hesitation, a preference, a disagreement, name it immediately with warmth. Over time, this teaches the nervous system that authenticity is safer than performance in this particular relationship.

Understand that progress with a fawn response can look like the relationship getting harder before it gets easier. As the person begins to trust that they are genuinely safe, the agreeable surface will start to crack. They may become more honest, which can include more critical. They may say no for the first time. These are not signs that the relationship is deteriorating. They are signs that it is becoming real. Real is what heals.

CHAPTER FOURTEEN

Holding a Disclosure

A disclosure is not information being shared. It is a body being entrusted. Handle accordingly.

What Disclosure Costs the One Disclosing

When someone opens their mouth to tell you something they have been carrying, their nervous system pays a price. The protective architecture around the story has to loosen. Old fear rises. Shame often rises with it. Many people will feel physically sick during or after a disclosure. Many will not sleep well that night. Many will pull back from you for days afterward, unsure what was given and what was taken.

Your understanding of this cost will shape how you hold what they give you. Treat every disclosure like the body on the other side has spent something real to offer it. Because it has.

The First-Time Disclosure

The first-time disclosure is any moment when a person is telling their story to another human for the first time. Sometimes the story is old. Sometimes it is fresh. Either way, the first telling carries weight the second and third tellings will never carry again.

What happens in the body of the person disclosing for the first time is often violent. They may feel unreal. They may feel as though they are watching themselves speak from across the room. They may forget parts of what they said five minutes after saying it. They may tremble. They may apologize for telling you. They may say they are fine when they are clearly not.

What you do in this moment will be woven into their memory of the telling. If you receive them well, the telling becomes part of their healing. If you receive them badly, the telling becomes part of the trauma. The stakes are that real.

The Protocol for a First-Time Disclosure

- Slow everything down. Your pace teaches theirs.
- Say thank you. Thank you for trusting me. Name the trust. Make it visible.
- Believe them. You are not the investigator. You are the witness. Belief is the first medicine.
- Stay close. Physically stay in the room. Emotionally stay in the room. Do not look at your phone. Do not check the time.
- Ask only what they invite. Do you want to say more? is a question. Tell me what happened is a demand dressed as a question.
- Say I am sorry that happened to you. Say it plainly. Do not inflate it. Do not diminish it.
- Close the conversation gently. Do not let it end abruptly. Mark it: thank you for telling me. I am going to keep holding this with care.
- Follow up the next day. Not to press. Just to show that the door stays open.

Words That Land at a First-Time Disclosure

- Thank you for trusting me.
- I am here. Take your time.
- You do not have to say more than you want to say.
- I am so sorry that happened to you. I am glad you are telling me.
- I believe you.

Words That Harm at a First-Time Disclosure

- Are you sure that is what happened?
- Why did you not tell anyone before now?
- Why did you not just leave?
- Well, they were going through a hard time.
- At least it was not worse.
- Everything happens for a reason.

Sexual Assault or Abuse Disclosure

Sexual assault disclosures carry their own architecture. Shame is almost always present. Self-blame is almost always present. The survivor will often be watching your face carefully, checking whether the telling is safe. A single shift in your expression can close the door.

You do not need to know the legal definitions. You do not need to know the statistics. You need to know this: their body is offering you something it has likely been holding alone for a long time. Your job is to make the room safe enough that the telling can happen.

What Survivors Most Often Need from the First Supporter

- To be believed, without questioning or clarification seeking.
- To have their sense of reality confirmed. What happened to you was real.
- To be told clearly that it was not their fault. Say it plainly. Say it again.
- To not be asked about physical details, the perpetrator's motivation, or what they were wearing, drinking, or doing.
- To be asked what they need rather than told what to do.
- To retain full agency about any next steps, including reporting. Reporting is not your decision. It is theirs.

- To know that you will hold this in confidence unless they ask you to share.

The Agency Principle

A sexual assault is, at its core, a violation of agency. Another person took control of a body without its consent. Any response from you that reintroduces a loss of control, even in the name of helping, can retrigger the original wound. This is why telling them what to do, calling the police without asking, or deciding who else should know can feel like another harm.

The survivor is sovereign. Every move you make should reinforce their sovereignty. Your role is to offer options, not directions.

Active Suicidality

The moment someone tells you they do not want to be alive is a moment that can save or lose a life. This is the single most frightening disclosure most of us will ever receive. Your fear is appropriate. Your shaking hands are appropriate. And you can still do this.

Every widely taught gatekeeper program, from QPR to ASIST to SafeTALK, rests on the same few principles. Ask directly. Do not leave. Get help on the way.

What to Do When Someone Tells You They Are Thinking of Ending Their Life

- Stay calm on the outside. Your steadiness lends them steadiness.
- Thank them for telling you. This is the bravest sentence they have ever spoken aloud.
- Ask directly. Are you thinking about ending your life? Do you have a plan? Do you have access to what you would use? The research is clear: asking directly does not plant the idea. Asking directly saves lives.

- Stay with them. Do not leave the room. Do not send them home alone. Do not hang up the phone.
- Get help moving toward them. Offer to call a crisis line together. Offer to call their therapist. Offer to call a family member. If they have a plan and access to means, call 988 or your country's equivalent immediately.
- Remove access to means if possible, in a way that preserves their dignity.
- Stay until safety is in place. Another trusted person or a professional has taken the relay.
- Follow up. Call the next day. Call the day after. Your presence in the days following is protective.

Words That Land at a Disclosure of Suicidality

- I am so glad you told me. I want to stay right here with you.
- I do not want to lose you. Will you let me help you call someone who can hold this with us?
- You do not have to figure this out alone. There are people who are trained for exactly this, and they want to be with you too.
- I believe you that this hurts. I also know this pain is not the whole truth, and I want to be beside you while we find the rest of it.

Crisis resources for this chapter and all others are gathered in Appendix C.

Flashback, Dissociation, or Panic in Real Time

Sometimes the disclosure is not words. Sometimes it is the body doing something the person cannot control in your presence. A flashback. A dissociative episode. A panic attack. They may look far away, or frozen, or suddenly terrified by something you cannot see.

How to Recognize What You Are Seeing

- Flashback: the person seems to be somewhere else, possibly reliving a past event. Their eyes may be unfocused or locked on something invisible.
- Dissociation: the person seems absent, flat, disconnected from their body. They may speak in a monotone. They may say I am not here.
- Panic attack: rapid breathing, racing heart, trembling, a sense of impending doom. They may feel like they are dying or going crazy. They are not. Their nervous system is in full sympathetic activation.

What to Do in the Moment

- Speak softly and slowly. Your voice is the rope.
- Name the present moment gently. You are safe. You are in my kitchen. It is Tuesday. The sun is out. Your body is here.
- Invite their senses to orient. Can you name five things you can see? Four things you can hear? Your feet on the floor? The chair holding you?
- Offer something physical if welcome. A glass of cold water. An ice cube. A textured object to touch.
- Breathe with them. Slow, audible exhales. Their body may borrow your rhythm.
- Wait. A flashback ends. A dissociative episode ends. A panic attack ends. Your steady presence is what closes it.

Disclosure of Harm by a Family Member

This is one of the hardest disclosures to receive, because the person being named is often also loved. The impulse to defend, to minimize, to ask for the other side, to shift the story into something more tolerable is enormous. You will have to fight that impulse in your own body.

The survivor is not asking you to choose sides. They are asking you to believe them. Believing someone does not require you to stop loving the other person. It requires you to hold what is true.

Domestic Violence and Coercive Control

Coercive control is a pattern of domination through fear, isolation, surveillance, financial control, and emotional manipulation. It may or may not include physical violence. It is often the slow narrowing of a life. The person living inside it often does not see the full shape until they are well out of it, and sometimes not even then.

If a client is disclosing coercive control, the most important thing to understand is this: telling them to leave often pushes them further in. Abusers watch for outside influences. A supporter who demands action can become a threat the abuser uses to cut off further contact.

What the Person in a Controlling Relationship Needs

- A door that stays open no matter how long the leaving takes. On average, a person leaves a controlling relationship seven times before leaving for good. Do not count.
- To be believed without having to prove the severity.
- To retain control over the timing of any safety plan.
- To know about resources without being ordered to use them.
- Your patience. The leaving is a nervous system event, not a decision.

Grief Disclosure

Grief is the most universal disclosure. Every facilitator will meet it. The person who has lost a human, a pet, a home, a pregnancy, a dream, a relationship, a body, a career, or a sense of the future is carrying something the surrounding culture does not know how to hold.

Grief is not a problem. Grief is love with nowhere to go. It is a natural and healthy response to the end of something that mattered. Treat it with the same respect you would treat love, because it is love.

The Common Harms at Grief

- Rushing someone through it. They are in a better place is almost never comforting.
- Comparing their grief to others. At least you had them for so long.
- Offering silver linings. This will make you stronger.
- Disappearing after the first week. Grief goes on. The casseroles stop. The calls stop. The body grieves alone.
- Forcing them back to normal on your timeline rather than theirs.

Words That Land at Grief

- I am so sorry.
- I do not have the right words. I just wanted you to know I am thinking of you.
- Tell me about them.
- I am not going anywhere. Grief takes the time it takes.
- What would feel good today? A walk? Silence? Nothing?

The Responsibility Held by the Safe Person

A disclosure lands. The space between you and the person in front of you changes shape. You are holding something sacred now, and that is relational power. It is responsibility of what is next. If there is harm to themselves or others named, you are legally obligated to report.

Trauma does not live in a certain body, class, or neighbourhood. If you work with humans, you work with people carrying trauma. Coaching calls, yoga classes, circles, teams, classrooms, groups. Every room with nervous systems is already a room where trauma is present. Being trauma-informed is the baseline for being a safe person in any of them.

Disclosure is a matter of when. Sometimes the person has rehearsed it for years. Sometimes it surprises them as much as it surprises you. Their nervous system has been waiting for someone attuned, and in that moment, you have become the one. Once you are attuned, the disclosures will happen because their nervous system calms and opens.

How you respond sets the tone for what it means, for them, to reveal a reality they have carried alone. If you flinch, collapse, or rush to fix, the body files that away. If you stay, soften, breathe with them, and let silence hold, that body learns it is possible to be heard.

Preparation is part of the responsibility. Know the trauma-informed practitioners and first responders in your area before you need them. Therapists who work somatically, Indigenous counsellors, culturally specific supports, crisis lines, bodyworkers who hold trauma consciously, social workers, etc. Build the map before the moment.

CHAPTER FIFTEEN

The Session: From Opening to Closing with Care

A trauma-informed session is a carefully tended arc. It has a beginning that lands, a middle that breathes, and an ending that honours.

Opening the Session

- Begins with arrival, not content: give people a moment to land in the room and in their bodies
- Acknowledges that being present took something: courage, time, trust
- Orients people to the space: what will happen, approximately how long, what is available to them
- Names the **safer space** agreements and invites participation in their refinement
- States the right to withdraw explicitly and warmly
- Offers a **grounding** invitation: a breath, a body scan, a moment of settling

Words That Open the Room: Practitioner Scripts

The words we speak at the threshold of a session carry power. They set the temperature of the room. They tell people, through language and breath and presence, whether this is a space where they can be whole.

The opening script is not a perfunctory greeting. It is an invocation. It is the practitioner saying, out loud, that this room has been built with intention.

What follows are three opening scripts: one for individual sessions, one for virtual work, and one for group circles. They are just examples for you to draw from and if you choose you can read them aloud before you use them. Let them land in your own body first. Adapt them. Make them true to how you speak.

Script for One-on-One Sessions

"Welcome. I am grateful you are here. This is a space I have prepared specifically for you, for this work we will do together. I want you to know from the beginning that this is your time, and your experience is the centre of what happens here.

What we do in this space is rooted in several things. First, we work from the knowing that you are whole. You are not broken. Your responses to the world have made sense given where you have been. That makes you sane. That makes you human.

Second, you are the expert on you. I am here to witness, to reflect, to ask questions that might open new territory. If at any point something does not feel right, if you need to slow down or pause or step away, that is your right and your responsibility to yourself. Say it. I will listen.

Third, there is no timeline on healing. You might feel a lot. You might feel nothing. You might feel something unexpected. All of that is exactly right.

Before we begin, I want to ground us both. Let us take three breaths together. Feel your feet on the floor. Feel the chair holding you. Feel the air moving in and out of your body. When you are ready, let me know where you want to start today."

Script for Virtual Sessions

"Thank you for showing up today. I know virtual work requires something of us: the presence to be here, the trust to let me see you through a screen, the willingness to work even though we are not in the same physical space. That takes courage.

This is still sacred space. The fact that we are separated by distance does not change what we are building here together. Your experience still matters. Your pace still matters. Your right to pause, to step away, to ask for a moment still stands.

I ask that your camera stays on so I can read your face and your expressions. That is how I witness you well. If at any point you need to step away from the screen, just send me a quick message first so I know you are alright.

If you need to move around, to stand, to shake out your body, to cry, to be still, do it. Your body is part of this work. Honour it.

Let us arrive together. Close your eyes if that feels okay. Notice where your feet are. Notice your breath. When you are ready, open your eyes and let me know where we are starting today."

Script for Group and Circle Sessions

"Welcome. I want to say this clearly and from my heart: you matter. The fact that you are here, that you showed up, that you are willing to be in this circle and do this work together, that matters.

This is a circle where you are seen. Where your experience is valid. Where emotion is welcome. Where silence is respected. Where you are not required to perform or fix or manage anyone else's experience. Your only job is to tend to yourself.

We will be talking about things that matter. Things that might be tender. Things that live in the body and the heart and the nervous system. Some of what you hear might land deeply. Some of it might not be for you right now. That is all okay.

What is spoken here stays here. You get to participate exactly as you need to. You have the right to pass. If you need to step out of the circle for any reason, you can do that. We will hold the circle for you.

Let us arrive together. Close your eyes. Feel your feet on the ground. Let your breath find its natural rhythm. When you are ready, open your eyes, and we will begin."

During the Session: Maintaining the Container

- Check in visibly and verbally at transitions
- Pace the content to the room, not to the agenda

- Name what you are observing without diagnosing
- Keep your own nervous system in view. If you feel anxious about the time or the agenda, that will broadcast. Breathe first.
- Celebrate every authentic response, including no, I do not want to, and I am not ready

The Sacred Art of Witnessing Emotion

This is the heart of the work. This is where facilitators either become instruments of healing or, often unconsciously, instruments of shutdown. The difference lies entirely in the facilitator's relationship to other people's emotions and their consciousness of where that relationship comes from.

Many facilitators, even experienced ones, have a pattern: when someone begins to cry, when sadness deepens, when anger rises, when grief moves through the room, the impulse to comfort springs up immediately. The urge to soothe. To touch. To offer tissues. To redirect, to move through the emotion efficiently, to get to the other side.

This impulse is not coming from a place of cruelty. It is coming from a place of the facilitator's own discomfort. When you watch someone cry, your own nervous system registers that as a threat. Your own relationship to pain, your own unprocessed grief begins to activate. And your nervous system wants that sensation to stop. So you reach for comfort. You reach for fixing.

This is one of the most insidious ways we shut down healing without even realizing it. We are consoling someone out of their own process in order to console ourselves.

Know Your Own Relationship to Emotion

Before you can safely hold another person's emotion, you must know your own. You must know where your tolerance ends. You must know what emotions activate you.

Some facilitators cannot hold grief. Some cannot hold anger. Some cannot hold silence. You must know these things about yourself. You must have done your own work. This is the foundation of being able to hold space for other people's emotions.

The Impulse to Comfort Is About You

If someone is crying, let them cry. Tears are the body's release mechanism. Tears are how the nervous system moves from contraction to expansion. When you interrupt tears, you are stopping the very biological process that is healing the person.

Your job is not to fix the tears. Your job is to make it safe for the tears to come. To say with your presence: "You are okay. Your body is doing exactly what it needs to do right now. I am here. I am not alarmed. You are safe to feel this."

Many people will apologize when they cry. They grew up in homes where emotion was not permitted. One of the most powerful things you can say is: "You have nothing to apologize for. This is welcome here."

Emotions as Part of the Human Spectrum

There is a profound teaching in the concept of taste. Humans have five taste receptors: sweet, salty, sour, bitter, and umami. We do not go through life trying to eliminate the sour or the bitter. We understand that the full range creates a complete sensory experience.

Emotions are the same. Joy. Grief. Rage. Fear. Love. Shame. Delight. Despair. None of them are bad. What matters is how we move through them. How we metabolize them.

Most people grew up in systems that asked them to eliminate certain emotions. What this does is dam up the emotion. It goes underground. It becomes the **traum-our**, the protective armour we build. It gets stored in the body. It emerges as disease, as numbness, as addiction, as **dysregulation**.

When you create a space where all emotions are welcome, you are offering something most people have never experienced. You are saying: all of you is welcome. All of you.

Titration: Holding the Group While Honouring the Individual

If one person's emotional process is consuming all the group's energy, you need to gently titrate. You might say: "Your process is real and important and welcome. I want to make sure we can also hold space for others in the circle. Would you be willing to take this to the side with our co-facilitator for a few minutes?"

The co-facilitator steps out with the person to continue the process in a different **container**. This is consciousness about how to hold everyone.

The Generational Truth

Many people alive today are the first in their family lines to have a space where they can safely feel. Where emotion is not pathologized. Where sadness is not seen as depression. Where anger is not seen as dangerous.

This stored, suppressed emotion lives in the bodies of millions of people. When you create a space where people can feel, you are creating healing. The tears that flow, the rage that comes, the grief that moves through the body: these are the beginning of liberation.

The person sitting in front of you, crying, may never have had a safe, loving space to feel before. This moment may be generationally significant. That is sacred. Hold it with the reverence it deserves.

That is the sacred art of witnessing emotion. That is how we help reweave the generational pattern, one felt experience at a time.

Closing the Session

The closing of a session is as important as the opening. For a person who has gone into vulnerable territory, being dropped at the end without proper closure can re-activate the nervous system and undo some of the safety built during the session.

- Allow adequate time: at minimum fifteen to twenty minutes for a standard session
- Invite a return to the body: grounding, breath, a slow noticing
- Create space to name what is being carried forward and what is being left in the room
- Name clearly what **aftercare** is available and how to access it
- For groups, include a closing ritual that honours the collective

PART FIVE

The Textures of the Work

• • •

Some feelings move through a room before anyone speaks their name.

Shame, which makes people disappear inside their own skin. Grief, which is slow and sacred and often mistaken for something else. The particular pain of kindness landing on a body that was taught to brace for the next hit. Confusion. Relief so overwhelming it looks like collapse. Joy that arrives with tears and nobody knows why.

These are the textures. They do not follow the curriculum. They are the affects that ride along with trauma and the conditions around it, and they ask something specific of the witness.

These chapters sit with them. Name them. Teach you to stay. The sacred witness is the witness who does not flinch from the textures. These chapters are how you become that.

CHAPTER SIXTEEN

When Kindness Is Triggering: Trust, Safety, and Self-Regulation

Kindness can be threatening. Care can activate a **fight response**. Warmth from a practitioner can genuinely feel dangerous to someone whose experience of care has always come wrapped in conditions, manipulation, or eventual harm.

When the Body Does Not Know How to Receive Kindness

For someone who grew up in an environment where love was unpredictable, conditional, or weaponized, unconditional positive regard can feel profoundly disorienting. The nervous system has learned to read safety through patterns. And if the pattern of the past was 'when someone is kind, something is about to cost me,' then your kindness becomes a signal of incoming threat.

This person may test you. They may push back without visible reason. They may challenge your competence, create conflict, arrive late, or disappear. None of this is about you. It is the nervous system doing exactly what it has always done: probing for the crack in the kindness.

When this happens, the most healing thing you can do is refuse to take the bait. Stay warm. Stay consistent. Stay honest. Let your steadiness be the message.

Self-Regulation as Your Primary Skill

When someone is in a stress response in your space, your nervous system is the most powerful intervention available to you. Before any technique, before any words, your regulated nervous system reaching toward their dysregulated one is what creates the possibility of **co-regulation**.

- Deliberately slowing your own breath when you feel the room activate
- Softening your face, particularly your eyes and the muscles around your mouth
- Lengthening the exhale, which activates the **parasympathetic nervous system**
- **Grounding** your feet intentionally into the floor
- Slowing your speech and lowering your vocal register
- Resisting the urge to fill silence immediately

Steady Is the Medicine: The Glimmer You Become

You will sit with humans whose trauma is more complicated than any framework can hold. Complex post-traumatic stress. Layered intergenerational pain. Body-level memory from events they cannot name because they were pre-verbal when the imprint was set. Dissociative systems that formed to keep a child alive. Religious trauma braided with family trauma braided with cultural trauma braided with the everyday wear of living in a body the world has not made safe.

Here is a truth that may come as a relief. You do not need to know the whole story. You do not need to trace the origin of every wound. You do not need to map the complexity. You will not be able to, and that is not the job.

Your job is to be the steady thing in a life that has not known many steady things.

Consistency Is Its Own Medicine

The body keeps its own records. Long before the conscious mind has settled whether a person is safe, the nervous system has been tracking. Same voice, same way. Same warmth, same patience. The same pair of eyes that did not flinch when something hard was spoken. Week after week, call after call, check-in after check-in. The body builds a file labeled this one has not left yet. Every return updates the file. The file, over time, becomes a new felt possibility.

The person in front of you is not keeping track of whether your words were brilliant. They are tracking whether you can be relied on. You may not be conscious of being tracked. They may not be conscious of tracking. It is happening anyway, in the layer below language, where the nervous system does its slow math about who is safe.

Consistency across time is a language the body believes more than words. Show up. Show up again. Show up the next time. The medicine lives in the repetition.

You Do Not Have to Understand It to Hold It

There is a particular fear that hits new witnesses when the story being shared is bigger than their understanding. If I do not fully get it, I will do harm. If I do not know the exact category of this trauma, I will miss something important. If I have not read the book, taken the course, received the certification, I should not be in this seat.

That fear is honest. It is also, most of the time, wrong. What the person in front of you needs is not for you to understand their trauma. What they need is for you to not need to understand their trauma in order to stay with them. The moment understanding becomes the price of your presence, their body knows. Their body has seen that trade before. They will shrink to fit what you can handle. The medicine collapses.

If you do not understand, say so. I do not fully understand what you just shared. I am still with you. Tell me what you need right now.

That sentence will do more than a hundred informed responses that were never asked for. It gives the person back the thing trauma usually steals, which is agency over their own story.

The Glimmer You Become

A glimmer, as Deb Dana named it, is a micro-moment in which the nervous system registers safety. A specific signal in the environment that the body reads as good. For a person whose life has sent mostly danger signals, a glimmer is not just a good feeling. A glimmer is a doorway. It tells the body, quietly, that other safety might be possible too.

Sometimes your role in someone's life becomes a glimmer. Not because you said the right thing. Not because you had the right framework. Because you were the person who kept showing up. Your voice, over time, becomes a sound their nervous system associates with settling. Your presence becomes a signal the body reads as we are okay here. Your consistency becomes a doorway.

You will usually not know when you are being someone's glimmer. You will think you are just showing up, just doing the small thing, just being ordinary. And their body will be quietly using you to relearn that being seen does not have to hurt. That someone can stay. That some people come back. That the old story is not the only story their body is allowed to hold.

This is why you do not need to fix. You do not need to solve. You do not need to know the complexities. You need to be consistent. You need to be steady. You need to return. The nervous system across from you is not asking for your brilliance. It is asking for your reliability. That is a far lower bar, and a far deeper gift, than most of us were taught to believe.

When you become a glimmer in someone's life, you are not doing the healing. You are opening a door the healing can walk through.

Rest into this. Let it take the pressure off. You are not trying to be a trauma expert. You are trying to be a steady human in relationship with another human. Steady is the medicine. Steady is the doorway. Steady is what lets something new become possible for a body that had stopped imagining new was an option.

That is the whole practice. Now go be that, for the next person who comes.

CHAPTER SEVENTEEN

Shame, Grief, and the Affects That Ride Along

Shame is the fear of disconnection. Grief is love that cannot reach its object. Both are responses to belonging lost or threatened. Both ask to be received, never corrected.

Shame Is the Water Most Disclosures Swim In

Brené Brown distinguishes guilt from shame in a way that has reshaped the conversation. Guilt says I did something bad. Shame says I am bad. Guilt can be a useful signal. Shame is almost always distorted. And shame is the current that runs through most trauma disclosures, especially those involving abuse, assault, addiction, or perceived failure.

A person held in shame cannot receive care, because they do not believe they deserve care. Their body is braced for the withdrawal they expect. If you arrive with love and the shame has not softened, the love bounces off. You will sometimes feel, sitting with a client, that your care is falling into a hole and nothing is landing. That hole is shame.

Your job as facilitator is not to argue with the shame. Arguing with shame makes it louder. Your job is to stay present to the human underneath the shame and wait for the human to notice you are still there.

How Shame Shows Up in the Body

- Eyes that cannot meet yours. A head that drops.
- Shoulders that curl inward. A chest that caves.
- A voice that goes small or disappears mid-sentence.

- Skin that flushes.
- A sudden joke or deflection. Humour is one of the most common shame armors.
- Disappearing from the conversation. Saying it is fine, it is not a big deal, I should not have said anything.

What Shame Needs from a Facilitator

- Steady eye contact without staring. Let your gaze be soft and available.
- A voice that does not rise or sharpen.
- Silence that is warm, not cold.
- Statements that undo the isolation. You are not alone. Many people carry this. I am still here.
- Restraint from reassurance that flattens. You are so amazing, do not feel bad can sometimes make shame worse because it rushes past the actual ache.
- Shared humanity. Shame feels impossible when it is believed to be uniquely shameful.

Self-Compassion as the Direct Antidote

Kristin Neff has given the field its cleanest articulation of self-compassion. Three components: mindfulness (noticing that suffering is present, without pushing it away and without drowning in it), common humanity (remembering that this suffering is part of the human condition), and self-kindness (offering oneself the same warmth one would offer a friend).

A facilitator teaches self-compassion by modelling it. When you meet a client's shame, the language you offer is the language they will eventually use on themselves. The phrases you use in this conversation become the inner voice they carry forward.

Try this. When a client describes a moment of private shame, say gently: what would you say to a dear friend who told you what you just told me? Almost always, they will offer their imaginary friend much more kindness than they have offered themselves. Then you can say: can you hear yourself saying those same words to the part of you that lived through this?

Grief Is the Other Underground River

Every disclosure carries a grief. The grief of what was taken. The grief of who you could have been. The grief of the years spent carrying what should have been witnessed long ago. The grief of the part of yourself that did not survive. Even a story told a hundred times carries the same grief at the hundredth telling, because grief does not shorten. It only widens the body's capacity to hold it.

Francis Weller writes of five gates of grief. Reading them slowly changes how a facilitator listens.

The Five Gates of Grief, Adapted from Francis Weller

- Gate one. The losses we know and name. A person who died. A relationship that ended. A home that burned.
- Gate two. The places in us that have not known love. The parts of ourselves we hid, abandoned, or were taught to be ashamed of. The grief of the unloved self.
- Gate three. The sorrows of the world. The grief we carry as members of a species and a planet in crisis. Climate. War. Displacement.
- Gate four. What we expected and did not receive. The parents we needed. The community we were promised. The safety a child has the right to expect and often does not get.
- Gate five. Ancestral grief. The unmourned losses of those who came before us. The wars our grandmothers survived and never spoke of. The displacements. The silences.

When you witness a grief, it often belongs to more than one gate. A client disclosing childhood abuse may be at gate four, gate two, and gate five at once. You do not need to sort the gates. You need to know that grief is this wide, and to let it be this wide in your witnessing.

Grief Is Not a Problem

The culture around you will treat grief as a problem. It will try to fix it, rush it, explain it, moralize it, or distract from it. You are not required to participate.

Grief is the body's honouring of what mattered. A body that does not grieve is a body in shutdown. The grief is part of the love. The two are the same substance in different seasons.

Disenfranchised Grief

Some griefs the world does not know how to honour. The death of a pet. The loss of a pregnancy. The estrangement from a family member who is still alive. The end of a relationship others did not recognize. The slow loss of a parent to dementia. The loss of a role. The loss of a body part, a function, a capacity. These are called disenfranchised griefs, and they are carried mostly in silence because the culture does not offer a ritual.

The facilitator of disenfranchised grief offers the acknowledgement the culture withholds. This is a real loss. This deserves grief. I will honour this with you.

Ambiguous Loss

Pauline Boss named a particular kind of loss. Ambiguous loss. When the loss has no clear end or confirmation. The missing person. The alienated family member. The parent with Alzheimer's who is physically present and psychically gone.

Ambiguous loss is harder to grieve because it does not resolve. The body cannot complete the mourning. For the facilitator, the work is naming the ambiguity itself. You are grieving something that is still here and also not here. That is exhausting, and there is no resolution coming.

The Other Affects That Ride Along

Anger

Anger is not a problem. Anger is often the first sign of healing. A person in fawn or freeze who starts to feel anger is often beginning to come back to themselves. The task is to welcome anger without flinching, while keeping safety. You are allowed to be this angry. It makes sense.

Numbness

Numbness is a message. The body has decided that feeling is more than it can afford right now. Do not try to force feeling. Sit with the numbness. Ask what it is protecting. Often, beneath numbness is a grief that would take a person to their knees. The numbness is the body's way of remaining upright.

Relief

Sometimes a disclosure brings relief, and the person feels guilty about the relief. They may apologize for feeling okay. Receive their relief as real. Relief is part of the metabolizing. It is a signal that something has been put down.

Love

Often, even in the presence of immense harm, the survivor still loves the person who harmed them. This is real. It is confusing to the facilitator. Honour it. I know you still love them. This does not cancel what they did. Both are true.

Being a Mirror: Where Shame and Grief Begin to Loosen

Everything this chapter has named is heavy. Shame, grief, rage, despair, the loneliness that rides along beneath them all. You will hold humans through these affects and you will not be able to pull the knots apart for them. That is not the job, and it was never going to be the job. No one is coming with a clever sentence that takes shame off a body. No one is coming with a bright idea that lifts grief out of a life. The disentangling belongs to the person, to time, and to the slow relational work of being held.

Your role is something older and smaller and more powerful. You are the mirror. The kind of mirror that reflects back what has always been whole underneath the wound. You are the witness who sees them without turning away when the shame rises. Who sees them without shrinking their grief. Who sees them without flinching when the rage becomes a sound. The mirror does not fix. The mirror reflects. The mirror reminds the body that it is still here, still a self, still someone worth staying with.

There is a specific kind of comfort that comes from being seen. Seen without being analyzed. Seen without being summarized. Seen. The person does not need you to understand their pain perfectly. They need you to believe that their pain is real, that they are still a whole human underneath it, and that they are worth staying with while it moves. Your belief, held steadily, is what they borrow until their own belief comes back online.

Your Presence Is the Promise of the Other Side

You will feel the urge to say something that communicates hope. Most of the time, you will not need to. The felt experience of being witnessed without judgment is already its own message to the nervous system. You are not alone. Something on the other side of this is possible.

The person reads hope in your breathing more than in your words. They read it in the fact that you did not leave. They read it in your willingness to sit with their pain without trying to turn it into something else. Your presence is already saying the thing you do not need to say out loud. There is a life on the other side of this. I am already sitting in part of it with you.

Hold the reflection long enough, and something in them begins to imagine the other side. Not as a destination you are selling. As a possibility their body can register because yours is embodying it. You are not the ending of their story. You are a mirror in which they begin to see that the story can keep unfolding.

Boundaries Do Not Mean We Do Not Love

If the work described in this chapter has started to feel too heavy, please hear this part carefully. Boundaries are not the opposite of love. Boundaries are what love requires from you in order to continue being love rather than slowly becoming something else.

A boundary is the practice of keeping yourself supported, attuned, and connected to your own life while you are in relationship with someone who is suffering. A boundary might be a limit on how many crisis texts you can receive between ten at night and six in the morning. It might be a session length you do not override. It might be a topic you send someone to a trained practitioner for. It might be a weekly practice you do not sacrifice no matter how many fires are happening in other lives. It might be a sentence that comes out of your mouth when the weight begins to tip. I love you, and I can hold this with you for twenty minutes tonight. Then I need to stop.

Boundaries are not rejection. Boundaries are the architecture that makes your ongoing presence possible. The alternative, the one so many helpers have tried, is to say yes to everything, absorb without limit, and slowly stop being able to stay. Collapse dressed up as love is no longer love. Sustainable, resourced presence is what love actually looks like when it plans to stay.

Boundaries mean we love ourselves enough to do whatever it takes to keep our own self supported, attuned, and connected. Find the practice. Find the person. Find the ritual. Find the practitioner. Find the community. Find the rest. Without that, the witnessing well runs dry, and the people who need you most will feel the absence when you have nothing left to give. With that, you can stay in this work for a lifetime.

Safe, Loved, and Protected

There is a line that bears returning to, because it names the nervous system truth under all of this. For anyone to feel open, curious, and connected, they must first feel safe, loved, and protected.

This is the physiological ground of everything this book has offered. The ventral vagal state, the social engagement system, the capacity to stay in connection, cannot come online in a body that does not feel safe. It cannot sustain itself in a body that does not feel loved. It cannot deepen in a body that does not feel protected. Safety, love, and protection are the soil. Openness, curiosity, and connection are what grows out of that soil.

This is true for the person you are witnessing. Your whole practice is building the conditions in which their body can feel safe, loved, and protected enough to begin opening. But it is also true for you. Your openness to their pain, your curiosity about their experience, your capacity to stay in connection with suffering, all depend on whether your own nervous system is receiving safety, love, and protection somewhere in your life. Boundaries are how you keep that supply alive. Relationships of mutual care are how you keep that supply alive.

Practice, land, community, rest, ancestry, and the return to your own body are how you keep that supply alive.

The most generous thing you can do for the person you witness is to remain whole enough to keep witnessing.

Love them. Mirror them. Sit in the hope their body cannot yet feel. And when it is time, put the work down. Tend to your own safety, your own loved, your own protected. Come back tomorrow. The circle is big enough to hold us all, and it is built to be walked in steadily, not carried alone.

PART SIX

Sustaining and Extending the Work

• • •

What you have built so far is a practice. What you need now is a life that can hold the practice.

How do you care for yourself and the person in your care after the session ends. How do you hold space on a screen without losing the somatic register. How do you continue this work across years, across many humans, across seasons in your own life when your capacity shifts.

These final chapters are about the long arc. The sustaining. The extending. The quiet protection of your own body so that the work has a body to come through.

The session ends. The work continues. This part shows you how to carry it.

CHAPTER EIGHTEEN

Aftercare, Follow-Up, and Caring for Yourself

The session ending does not mean the work is done. For the person you have been with, the hours and days that follow a deep facilitation experience can be some of the most tender and significant. For you, how you care for yourself after holding space determines how much you will have to offer the next time.

What Aftercare Is and Why It Matters

Aftercare is the intentional support offered to a person following a significant facilitation experience. Without it, people can feel stranded in the tender space that opens after deep work. They may be more emotionally raw than usual, more easily overwhelmed, less able to navigate daily demands.

Aftercare communicates: you are held even when you are not in the room with me.

Building Your Aftercare Practice

- A brief check-in message within 24 to 48 hours: 'I have been thinking of you. How are you landing?'
- Clear communication about how they can reach you if something significant surfaces
- Sharing one or two **grounding** practices they can use on their own between sessions
- Normalizing the **integration** process: 'It is completely normal for things to feel stirred up for a few days after deep work. That is the work working.'

Post-Session Checklist

Closing the Container

- ☐ Adequate closing time was held and not rushed
- ☐ A grounding or closing practice was offered
- ☐ Participants were oriented back to their day
- ☐ Aftercare information was provided clearly
- ☐ Space was made for any final questions or reflections

Aftercare and Follow-Up

- ☐ Follow-up contact timeline has been communicated
- ☐ Crisis resources have been shared if appropriate
- ☐ Participants know how to reach me between sessions if needed
- ☐ Any referrals needed have been identified and will be made within 24 hours

Practitioner Self-Care

- ☐ I have allowed transition time before my next obligation
- ☐ I have completed a somatic decompression practice
- ☐ I have noted anything I am carrying from this session that needs attention

A Framework for Practitioner Self-Care

Daily

- A **somatic** practice that grounds you in your body: movement, breath, cold water, time in nature
- A transition ritual that marks the end of your client-facing day
- Something that has nothing to do with healing work: creativity, pleasure, rest, play

Weekly

- Supervision or peer consultation, especially for heavy caseload.
- A practice that replenishes what the work draws from: deep rest, community, beauty, silence
- Honest reflection on your own **window of tolerance** and current capacity
- Monthly
- A review of your caseload and whether it is sustainable
- Time with your own practitioner, therapist, or healer
- Seasonally
- A genuine rest or retreat practice
- A revisitation of your intentions and your why
- Crisis resources shared proactively, especially after heavy session.

After the Witnessing

Your nervous system was built to hold other nervous systems, and it was also built to rest. The holding costs something, whether you feel it in the moment or not. When you sit with a client in her darkest hour, your body is doing the work of co-regulation, which means your system is taking some of the activation she is discharging. It lands in you. It has to go somewhere.

When this happens once, the body discharges and recovers. When it happens repeatedly without recovery, the body begins to carry the weight. Sleep gets thinner. Irritability rises. Joy flattens. You may begin to dread the phone call from the client who has always leaned hardest on you. You may begin to feel resentment you do not want to feel. You may begin to feel nothing at all, which is often the first sign of burnout.

This is the predictable cost of repeated witnessing without care. Laura van Dernoot Lipsky, in Trauma Stewardship, offers sixteen warning signs of what she calls trauma exposure response.

Sixteen Signs Your Body May Be Carrying Too Much

- Feeling helpless and hopeless.
- A sense that you can never do enough.
- Hypervigilance (constantly scanning for threat).
- Diminished creativity.
- Inability to embrace complexity. Everything feels black and white.
- Minimizing (my problems are nothing compared to what I just heard).
- Chronic exhaustion and physical ailments.
- Inability to listen, or deliberate avoidance of clients, friends, or family.
- Dissociative moments.
- A sense of persecution. Everyone is out to get me.
- Guilt, especially about your own good fortune.
- Fear for yourself and loved ones.
- Anger and cynicism.

- Inability to empathize or numbing.
- Addictions and numbing behaviours (alcohol, food, screens, overwork).
- A diminished sense of purpose or enjoyment.

If you recognize three or more of these in yourself, your body is telling you something. It is asking you to tend the container that holds the witnessing. Your body wants you to replenish so the work can continue.

The Practice of Aftercare

Aftercare is the deliberate, repeated practice of returning your nervous system to its baseline after holding another. It is as important as the witnessing itself. Aftercare operates in three timescales. The minutes after a session. The day after. The ongoing rhythm of your life.

In the Minutes After a Hard Session

- Move your body. Walk, stretch, shake. The activation that built up while you were still has to discharge.
- Drink cold water. The body metabolizes emotion with water.
- Wash your hands. Splash your face. The transition ritual matters to the nervous system.
- Make three slow exhales, longer than the inhales.
- Name out loud what just happened, at least to yourself. I just held something heavy. My body worked hard.
- Eat something. Trauma work depletes blood sugar.

In the Day After

- Sleep. Your system consolidates and metabolizes during sleep.
- Move. A walk, a yoga class, a swim. Movement completes what the body started.
- Talk to one trusted other human without breaking confidence.

- Eat simply and well. Warm foods. Bone broth. Vegetables your grandmother would have recognized.
- Limit inputs. Do not stack a hard witnessing day with doomscrolling.
- Allow a softer pace on the next day if you can.

In the Ongoing Rhythm of Your Life

- A weekly practice of embodied presence: yoga, somatic exercise, walking in nature, sweat, dance.
- A spiritual practice if it belongs to you. Prayer, meditation, ceremony, time with land.
- A peer. Someone you can call and say I held something heavy.
- Therapy or a skilled helper if the witnessing is stacking.
- A grief practice. You are witnessing real loss. Your body needs to grieve too.
- Joy that is deliberate, not accidental.

Ritual Closure After Witnessing

Many Indigenous and ancestral traditions teach that when a person holds another's pain, the holding must be closed with ritual. Without ritual closure, the energy can remain in the body or the home. This is not only metaphor. Traditional knowledge and contemporary somatic practice are in agreement on this.

A simple closing ritual after a heavy session:

- Wash your hands with warm water. As you wash, silently name what you are releasing. This is not mine to carry.
- If you have sage, cedar, sweetgrass, or palo santo, and it is appropriate for you, light it and pass the smoke through the space.
- Open a window for a few minutes. Let the room breathe.

- Place your hand on your own heart. Say silently: I am back in my own body. I bless the one I held. I give their story back to them.
- Drink a cup of warm tea slowly.

This takes five minutes. It changes what your body carries into the rest of your day.

Permission to Step Back

There will be seasons of your life when you cannot be a primary container. A death in your own family. A major illness. A collapse in your work or relationship. A phase of parenting that asks everything you have. A depression that arrives and lingers.

In those seasons, stepping back is wisdom. You are not abandoning your clients. You are protecting the long practice. A facilitator who burns out is unavailable for years. A facilitator who rests is available for decades.

Give yourself permission to say: I am in a hard season. I cannot hold as much right now. I will be back. The people who love you will receive this. The people who do not were always more transactional than loving. Their departure is information, not loss.

CHAPTER NINETEEN

Closing: Why Any of This Matters

The cost of not being trauma-informed is almost never dramatic. It is quiet. It compounds. It lasts generations.

You do not need to be convinced that doing harm is bad. No one who arrived at this book needed that education. What you may need, as you close the last chapters, is a clear-eyed accounting of what happens when the humans around a person in pain are not trauma-informed. Because most of the time, the harm is not loud. It is ordinary. It goes unnamed for years, sometimes across entire lifetimes, sometimes across whole lineages. Naming the cost out loud is how we refuse to pretend that being untrained is neutral.

Trauma-informed practice is not a specialty. It is a basic literacy for being in community with other humans. The sections that follow name the cost of treating it as optional.

The Child Who Tells and Is Not Believed

A nine-year-old girl finally tells a trusted adult that something has been happening at home. The adult, untrained, uncomfortable, overwhelmed, responds the way the dominant culture has taught most of us to respond. Are you sure? That does not sound like him. Do not say things like that, you will hurt people.

The child's nervous system records the outcome in a layer below language. Truth was spoken. Truth was punished. The body concludes that disclosure is dangerous. The abuse continues. The girl learns that her body is on its own.

Twenty years later, she is in therapy trying to understand why she cannot speak about what is happening in her current relationship. She does not consciously remember the moment at age nine. Her body remembers. The cost of the adult, back then, not being trauma-informed is an entire adulthood shaped by a silence that was installed in a child.

The Disclosure That Gets Pathologized

A man in crisis walks into a healthcare setting and describes feelings that, in context, are a predictable response to what he has lived through. Chronic grief after multiple losses. Nervous system activation after cumulative stress. Sleep disruption after trauma. The intake provider, working inside a system that rewards quick categorization, assigns a diagnosis and begins medication. The fact that his symptoms make sense given his history is never asked about.

The grief never gets grieved. The trauma never gets witnessed. He is told he has a chronic illness of his mind and is handed a plan that assumes the problem lives inside him, separate from story, separate from life. He leaves the appointment confirmed in the quiet suspicion he already held. Something is fundamentally wrong with me. The nervous system responses that were his body's intelligent adaptations are now reframed as symptoms of disease.

This is the dominant cultural reflex. It costs people their relationship with their own story.

The Indigenous Employee Asked to Educate

A non-profit rolls out equity training. In the middle of the session, the facilitator turns to the one Indigenous person in the room and says, can you share your perspective?

The employee smiles because she has been in this moment a thousand times. Inside her body, cortisol rises. She is now responsible for educating the people who have the power to promote her or to freeze her out. She chooses her words carefully. She makes everyone comfortable. She leaves the session more tired than when she arrived.

She adds this moment to the file her body keeps about what it costs to show up to work in this organization.

A year later she quits. The exit interview calls it pursuing other opportunities. The organization sends a note about how much she will be missed. They will not understand that they lost her because every attempt at doing the right thing was led by facilitators who had never been taught that asking her to perform her identity as a teaching tool was the exact thing she could no longer afford.

The Friend Who Leads With Fixing

A friend texts her sister that she is not okay. The sister responds with a well-meaning list. Have you tried therapy? Have you thought about journaling? I read an article about gratitude practices that I will forward you.

The friend reads the message, puts the phone down, and cries. She is lonelier now than she was before she texted. The next time she feels the edge of falling apart, she does not reach out. The cost is small in any single exchange. The cost, across a life, is a woman who stops asking for help because help has never felt like help.

The Leader Who Treats Boundaries as a Problem

A team member tells their manager that they cannot take on another project without something else coming off their plate. The manager, who has no framework for nervous system capacity, hears the boundary as a character issue. Over the following months, the team member begins to absorb subtle signals that they are no longer considered committed. Their assignments thin. Their inclusion in key conversations thins.

They burn out. They leave. The organization loses talent and institutional memory. A report is written about retention. The word trauma is never used. The pattern repeats with the next person. Then the next. The cost is a culture in which the only people who survive long term are the ones willing to override their own nervous systems, which is a selection pressure that guarantees the least attuned humans become the leaders.

The Collective Cost

Multiply every one of these stories by the number of humans alive right now. This is the cost of a world in which trauma-informed understanding is treated as optional specialty training rather than basic literacy for being in community with other humans.

It is a cost paid disproportionately by the people already carrying the most. It shows up as chronic illness, as addiction, as broken relationships, as systems that fail, as institutions that lose the people they claim to serve, as children who grow into adults still waiting for the moment when somebody stayed. It is the water most of us were raised swimming in. It is what we have been calling normal for so long that we have forgotten normal was a choice.

What Changes When We Choose Differently

When the adult believes the nine-year-old, the disclosure pathway stays open and the abuse has a chance to stop.

When the intake provider asks what happened to you instead of what is wrong with you, the grief becomes grief rather than a diagnosis, and healing becomes a road rather than a prescription.

When the facilitator prepares to teach the material herself rather than asking the one marginalized person in the room to teach for her, the Indigenous employee can stay. The organization keeps her wisdom. The training actually works, because the people in power are the ones being transformed.

When the friend says I love you, tell me more, before reaching for advice, the lonely sister knows she is not carrying it alone. The next text gets sent. The crisis does not compound in silence.

When the manager treats the boundary as useful information about human capacity, the team member stays, contributes, rests, and grows. Retention improves. Culture shifts. The next generation of leaders is shaped by a different pattern.

These are not dramatic changes. They are ordinary. They are within reach of the everyday witness. Every person who becomes trauma-informed becomes a break in a pattern that was going to continue. Every break in a pattern is a door that opens for the person whose life meets them next.

Why We Do This Work

We become trauma-informed because humans are already paying the cost of our not being trauma-informed, and most of them did not consent to pay it. We become trauma-informed because the alternative is that the suffering compounds generation by generation, and somebody has to decide to stop passing it down.

We become trauma-informed because there is a child, right now, waiting to be believed. There is a grieving man, right now, waiting to be witnessed. There is an Indigenous employee, right now, waiting for the meeting where nobody asks her to perform. There is a colleague, right now, waiting for a leader who reads a boundary as information. There is a friend, right now, holding her phone and wondering whether it is safe to send the text.

We will be one of the adults they meet. What kind of adult do we want to be?

The circle is widening because it has to. The cost of the alternative is too high. You have just spent nineteen chapters learning how to be the kind of witness whose presence lowers the cost for the person in front of you. That is the whole reason any of this matters.

The Spiral Path: Unlearning and Relearning

If this book has opened something in you, I want you to know that the opening is the beginning. The real work is a spiral. It moves inward first, into the places where your own story lives, where your own wounds have shaped how you hold others. And then it spirals outward again, into the rooms you enter, the circles you hold, the lives you touch. Inward and outward. Over and over. Each time deeper. Each time wider.

This is why I created *The Journey: A-Lion-Ment Path to Self-Actualization.* Because no matter who we are, no matter how many certifications we carry or how many years we have been in this work, we all benefit from knowing how to hold ourselves authentically so that we can hold others authentically. The Journey is that spiral path.

As someone who has held space across many seasons of this work, I want to share what I have come to know.

I first created space as a childbirth doula at twenty-one. Then I became a Reiki Master in my twenties, and it was during my yoga teacher training that I first heard the term "holding space." From there, I shared hundreds of one-on-one healing sessions, blending modalities as I went, and began hosting women's circles. I moved into professional leadership training, completed Life Skills Coach Training, and pursued my Master's degree with a specialization in trauma-informed practice for safe spaces. I became a college instructor. I became an educator within healthcare, holding space for some of the most tender material a human being can carry.

Across all of it, no matter the setting, no matter the title on the door, I began to see the same thing. There is a part of every person that longs to be seen. Truly seen. Witnessed in their authentic self. Some carry that hunger more visibly than others. And some have never once experienced being met in that place, because the roles they learned to express were shaped and defined by sources outside of them: their adaptive selves built to survive, not to be known.

These are my final thoughts about sharing safer space:

The people in your life are your sacred mirrors. Every relationship, every conflict, every moment of tenderness reflects something back to you about where you are in your own relationship with self. Even the challenging seasons, especially the challenging seasons, help you know who you truly are.

And here is what is beautiful about being someone who feels called to hold space for others: you get to witness the moments that most people never see. The moment someone's breath changes because something they have been carrying for decades just loosened its grip. The moment a person's eyes change, when the spark returns because something that was stifling them has finally been named and honoured and released.

That is a sacred honour. It is also a sacred responsibility.

We hold people in their process of pain and celebration. Of yearning and of releasing. Of joy and curious play and of huge, adventurous grit as they climb mountains that feel impossible to them. All of it. And when we are trying to do that safely, we do the best we can. We seek a commitment to that responsibility. We also release what is not ours to hold. Both are true at the same time.

None of us can get it right all the time. That is why we call them safer spaces. We strive for safer. We maintain the best we can through humility, courage, honesty, honour, and love.

When people feel and know you are genuinely holding them with dignity and respect, they can feel it. It is a felt, known embodiment. Something in their nervous system recognizes it, and for reasons that go deeper than language, they drop their guard. Sometimes it takes time. Like trust from an animal that has been hurt, they might need to see that we are the same consistent person over and over and over again. That is what it means to stay committed to being safe, regulated, connected.

And when we cannot, when we have grief, when our own foundation is cracking, it is the wise person who chooses to take a reprieve from holding space for others. That is wisdom. That is discernment. That is responsibility too.

When we hold too much and our foundation begins to fracture, that is when we must ask for help. Make sure you tell someone: I have taken on too much. None of us are meant to carry enormous amounts of suffering alone.

There is something many wounded healers move through: the idea that once you are wearing the hat of the helper, it means you can never need help. This is not true. The fear of not having it together, the ego of being not enough, this is one of the deepest traps in the healing professions. And it is one of the first things that must be healed.

There comes a moment of realization when we see that the very lens of pathologizing has been the hardwiring through which we have been viewing everything, including ourselves. The incredible expression of being here, of being alive, through all that your story is, that is the grace you also offer others.

People will only heal as far as your current state of freedom from your scars or core beliefs. Your healing embodiment to be authentic is their permission too. Generously give yourself grace to be this person entrusted by others. There is a deep commitment here. There is also a deep surrender.

Story is sacred. We all live in story. Part of unlearning is only possible when we also acknowledge the story that surfaces as we reclaim our parts. We must re-story our inner world, as it presents along the path, in the most loving way.

Nothing can ever be destroyed. This is energy. Emotion is immense energy. It can only ever be transformed. When someone re-stories with new eyes, we are space holders for them that are broadcasting a signal for their mirror neurons to attach a new lens. A lens of self-love.

However large the story, that same magnitude of energy tied to that emotion will be transformed. To contentment. To peace. To self-acceptance. To joy. To love. Our job is to hold the space, unconditionally loving, with boundaries that are solid. The transformation arrives in its own form and its own time. Like the riverbank. The riverbank does not try to direct the water. It is simply there, steady, solid, present. And because it is there, the river can flow. That is enough. You are enough.

Thank you for your dedicated commitment to wanting this world to become a healing planet. Thank you for doing the inner work so that the outer work can land with integrity. May we all see rivers running more and more clear. And may we enjoy that beauty together.

If you are ready to take the spiral path inward, *The Journey: A-Lion-Ment Path for Self-Actualization* is waiting for you. The Healership Academy is a Skool community for healers and leaders and change makers who are committed to this world of healing and who want to dance with their authentic selves and others. Visit www.simplysacred.ca to begin.

APPENDIX A

Trauma-Informed Language Quick Reference

Language is not neutral. What we say, how we say it, and what we choose not to say are all part of the container we build. This reference guide is designed to be returned to often.

Language Shifts for Trauma-Informed Practice

Avoid: "You need to talk about this."

Instead: "Whenever you feel ready, I am here to listen."

Choice is healing. Necessity replicates coercion.

Avoid: "I know how you feel."

Instead: "I can hear that this is really hard."

You cannot know. Claiming you do dismisses their uniqueness.

Avoid: "At least..." (silver lining)"

Instead: "That sounds incredibly painful."

Reframing too fast communicates their pain is inconvenient.

Avoid: "You should try to move on."

Instead: "Healing moves at its own pace. There is no timeline here."

Timelines for grief are a form of emotional coercion.

Avoid: "Have you tried just..."

Instead: "What has felt helpful for you in the past?"

Unsolicited advice implies their approach is wrong.

Avoid: "You are so strong."

Instead: "You are still here. That took something."

"Strong" can pressure people to suppress what they actually feel.

Avoid: "That must have been traumatic."

Instead: "How did that experience land for you?"

Let them name their own experience. Do not diagnose it.

Avoid: "Why did you let that happen?"

Instead: "None of this was your fault."

Why questions in crisis imply responsibility and shame.

Avoid: "Just breathe."

Instead: "If it feels okay, let us take one slow breath together."

Commands bypass consent. Invitations honour it.

Avoid: "I understand completely."

Instead: "Tell me more. I want to understand."

Claiming full understanding closes the conversation.

Avoid: "You are overreacting."

Instead: "Your response makes complete sense."

This is gaslighting. It is never appropriate.

Avoid: "Everyone goes through hard things."

Instead: "What you have been through is significant."

Minimizing through universalizing denies their particular pain.

Avoid: "Have you seen a therapist?"

Instead: "I want to make sure you have the right support. Can we talk about what that might look like?"

Unsolicited referrals can feel like rejection without context.

Avoid: "That was a long time ago."

Instead: "Time does not always change how something lives in the body."

Trauma is not linear. It does not age out.

Avoid: "You are so brave for sharing."

Instead: "Thank you for trusting me with that."

Brave implies their vulnerability is exceptional. Gratitude is warmer and more grounding.

APPENDIX B

The H.E.A.L. I.T. Framework

Everything in this book lives inside a larger container. A way of working, teaching, and building the kind of healing culture this book keeps pointing toward. That container has a name. H.E.A.L. I.T. Humility. Equity. Antiracism. Lateral Kindness. Inclusivity. Trauma-Informed.

H.E.A.L. I.T. is the framework I developed through Simply Sacred Solutions and now deliver through H.E.A.L. I.T. International. It is how I personally carry this work into rooms, into organizations, into systems. It is also how I teach it. The main delivery is a week-long training that walks participants through the full arc of becoming trauma-informed in practice. By the end, practitioners leave with language they can use on Monday, frameworks they can return to on Thursday, and a body that has been shown what this work feels like from the inside.

Alongside the week-long training, the work lives in two other offerings. Trauma-informed consultation for organizations, leaders, and teams who want to change culture from the ground up through a sustained relationship with someone who can see the patterns and help the container reshape. And The Healership Academy, a Skool community where practitioners gather for ongoing group mentorship, shared learning, and the kind of accountability that keeps the inner work moving long after any single training ends.

If you want to go deeper with any of this, the door is open. For certification in trauma-informed practices, for consultation with your organization, or to join the Healership Academy, reach out at simplysacred.coordinator@gmail.com.

Here they are explicitly named as they are built in the 6 sessions compassionate healership training:

H : Humility

The willingness to know that you do not know everything, and to hold your expertise loosely. Humility in healing work means staying curious, staying open, and never allowing your framework to override the sovereignty of the person in front of you.

E : Equity

Understanding that people arrive in your space from vastly different starting points shaped by systems, histories, and access. Equity means responding to what each person actually needs rather than offering the same thing to everyone and calling it fair.

A : Antiracism

Actively working to identify and dismantle the racial biases, assumptions, and systemic patterns that show up in healing spaces and in our own practice. This is ongoing work. It is never finished. We recognize that the dominant way of healing, being and doing life has been based in values mainly originating from Western Europe and we consistently ensure that this is not treated as superior.

L : Lateral Kindness

Care that flows between equals rather than down from authority. In healing spaces, lateral kindness means treating every person as a sovereign, capable human being, and creating conditions where people can also offer kindness to each other.

I : Inclusivity

Designing spaces, practices, and language that genuinely welcome the full range of human experience, identity, culture, and ways of knowing. Inclusivity recognizes that people may need accommodations to feel included and to belong and we recognize the deep intrinsic need we have as social mammals to connect and belong. We intentionally create space for this and ask people what they may need to experience more inclusion.

T : Trauma-Informed

Understanding trauma as a normal response to abnormal circumstances and designing every aspect of your practice to honour that understanding. That there may be experiences people are having that make them feel uncertain, in dysregulated states and that there are pathways to come back to regulation because of conscious approaches made.

APPENDIX C

Crisis Resources and Further Reading

Language around crisis support shifts as systems change. Verify any resource before passing it to a client. The most current source for Canadian resources is the Canadian Mental Health Association (cmha.ca). For United States resources, the Substance Abuse and Mental Health Services Administration (samhsa.gov).

Crisis Lines

Canada and the United States

- 988 Suicide and Crisis Lifeline (active in both Canada and the United States). Call or text 988.
- Talk Suicide Canada: 1-833-456-4566. Text 45645 (4 p.m. to midnight ET).
- Kids Help Phone (Canada): 1-800-668-6868. Text CONNECT to 686868.
- Hope for Wellness Helpline (Indigenous Canada): 1-855-242-3310. Online chat at hopeforwellness.ca.
- Trans Lifeline (Canada and United States): 1-877-330-6366 (Canada), 1-877-565-8860 (United States).
- Trevor Project (LGBTQ2S+ youth, United States): 1-866-488-7386. Text START to 678-678.
- Veterans Crisis Line (United States): dial 988, then press 1.
- Crisis Text Line (Canada): text HOME to 686868. (United States): text HOME to 741741.

Sexual Assault and Intimate Partner Violence

- RAINN National Sexual Assault Hotline (United States): 1-800-656-HOPE (4673).
- Ending Violence Association of Canada: endingviolencecanada.org.
- VictimLink BC (British Columbia): 1-800-563-0808.
- National Domestic Violence Hotline (United States): 1-800-799-7233. Text START to 88788.
- Assaulted Women's Helpline (Ontario): 1-866-863-0511.

Human Trafficking

- Canadian Human Trafficking Hotline: 1-833-900-1010.
- National Human Trafficking Hotline (United States): 1-888-373-7888. Text HELP to 233733.

Substance Use and Overdose

- SAMHSA National Helpline (United States): 1-800-662-HELP (4357).
- Canada-Wide Addiction and Mental Health Support: 1-866-585-0445.

Specialized Indigenous Resources

- Hope for Wellness Helpline: 1-855-242-3310.
- Indian Residential School Survivors Society (Canada): 1-800-721-0066.
- National Indian Residential School Crisis Line: 1-866-925-4419.
- Missing and Murdered Indigenous Women and Girls Crisis Line: 1-844-413-6649.

First-Response Training Worth Pursuing

If any part of this book has moved you to equip yourself further, consider:

- QPR (Question, Persuade, Refer). The most widely taught gatekeeper training for suicide prevention. Short, accessible, life-protective. qprinstitute.com.
- ASIST (Applied Suicide Intervention Skills Training), by LivingWorks. Two-day workshop. The deeper sibling of QPR.
- SafeTALK, also by LivingWorks. Half-day suicide alertness training.
- Mental Health First Aid (Canada and United States versions). Teaches a general first-response posture for mental health crises.
- Indigenous Cultural Safety training (San'yas, others). Essential complement for any facilitator working across cultural lines.

Voices Worth Adding to Your Shelf

Contemporary Trauma Foundations

- Menakem, R. My Grandmother's Hands: Racialized Trauma and the Pathway to Mending Our Hearts and Bodies. Central Recovery Press, 2017.
- Maté, G. The Myth of Normal: Trauma, Illness, and Healing in a Toxic Culture. Avery, 2022.
- Herman, J. Trauma and Recovery: The Aftermath of Violence. Basic Books, 1992 (updated 2015).
- Walker, P. Complex PTSD: From Surviving to Thriving. Azure Coyote, 2013.
- Perry, B. and Winfrey, O. What Happened to You? Conversations on Trauma, Resilience, and Healing. Flatiron Books, 2021.
- Dana, D. The Polyvagal Theory in Therapy: Engaging the Rhythm of Regulation. W. W. Norton, 2018.

- Schwartz, R. No Bad Parts: Healing Trauma and Restoring Wholeness with the Internal Family Systems Model. Sounds True, 2021.
- Hemphill, P. What It Takes to Heal: How Transforming Ourselves Can Change the World. Random House, 2024.
- Buqué, M. Break the Cycle: A Guide to Healing Intergenerational Trauma. Dutton, 2024.

Grief and Loss

- Weller, F. The Wild Edge of Sorrow: Rituals of Renewal and the Sacred Work of Grief. North Atlantic Books, 2015.
- Devine, M. It's OK That You're Not OK: Meeting Grief and Loss in a Culture That Doesn't Understand. Sounds True, 2017.
- Boss, P. Ambiguous Loss: Learning to Live with Unresolved Grief. Harvard University Press, 1999.

Indigenous Trauma and Healing

- Linklater, R. Decolonizing Trauma Work: Indigenous Stories and Strategies. Fernwood Publishing, 2014.
- Duran, E. Healing the Soul Wound: Counseling with American Indians and Other Native Peoples. Teachers College Press, 2006.
- Methot, S. Legacy: Trauma, Story, and Indigenous Healing. ECW Press, 2019.

Racialized Trauma Beyond Indigenous Contexts

- Mullan, J. Decolonizing Therapy: Oppression, Historical Trauma, and Politicizing Your Practice. W. W. Norton, 2023.
- Walker, R. The Unapologetic Guide to Black Mental Health. New Harbinger, 2020.

Gender, Sexuality, and Identity

- Real, T. I Don't Want to Talk About It: Overcoming the Secret Legacy of Male Depression. Scribner, 1997.
- Price, D. Unmasking Autism: Discovering the New Faces of Neurodiversity. Harmony, 2022.
- Vaid-Menon, A. Beyond the Gender Binary. Penguin Workshop, 2020.
- Piepzna-Samarasinha, L. L. Care Work: Dreaming Disability Justice. Arsenal Pulp Press, 2018.

Child and Adolescent Trauma

- Siegel, D. and Bryson, T. P. The Whole-Brain Child. Delacorte Press, 2011.
- Delahooke, M. Brain-Body Parenting. Harper Wave, 2022.

Witnessing Practice and Aftercare

- van Dernoot Lipsky, L. Trauma Stewardship: An Everyday Guide to Caring for Self While Caring for Others. Berrett-Koehler, 2009.
- Remen, R. N. Kitchen Table Wisdom: Stories That Heal. Riverhead Books, 1996.
- Neff, K. Self-Compassion: The Proven Power of Being Kind to Yourself. William Morrow, 2011.
- Brown, B. Daring Greatly. Gotham, 2012.

A Final Word on Resources

Resources change. Numbers change. Organizations are formed and dissolved. A living resource list needs living hands. At simplysacred.ca there is an ongoing page of verified resources updated throughout the year. Use it. Share it with the clients and communities you serve.

GLOSSARY

Key Terms and Definitions

Language shapes how we hold people. The terms in this glossary are the building blocks of trauma-informed practice. They are offered here so you can return to them as needed, grounding your understanding each time you revisit this work.

Activation: The state of the nervous system when it has detected a real or perceived threat. Activation is the body doing its job. It shows up as changes in breath, posture, voice, facial expression, and internal sensation. It is information, and it deserves to be read with care.

Aftercare: The intentional support offered to a person following a facilitation experience that touched something deep. Aftercare communicates that the relationship and the care extend beyond the walls of the session. It is how we say: you are still held.

Attunement: The practice of tuning your own nervous system to the frequency of another person's. Attunement is empathy made visible through presence, pacing, and the quality of your attention. It is one of the oldest forms of human medicine.

Bilateral Stimulation: Alternating sensory input between the left and right sides of the body. The foundational mechanism behind EMDR therapy. In this book, it refers primarily to the butterfly hug: crossing the arms over the chest and alternating gentle taps on the upper arms.

Buffer Time: Intentional pause built into a session after emotionally activating content. The nervous system needs time to integrate what it has just experienced. Buffer time looks like movement, breath, water, grounding. It is how we honour the body's need for oscillation between depth and surface.

Butterfly Hug: A bilateral tapping practice: crossing the arms over the chest and alternating taps on the upper arms or shoulders. A simple, portable tool for nervous system regulation that can be used in session or offered to a person as a self-soothing resource.

Ceremony: A vessel for transformation. Across cultures and throughout human history, ceremony has been the container in which humans metabolize experience, honour transitions, and return to themselves. In this book, it includes sweat lodges, vision quests, breathwork journeys, plant medicine experiences, and any practice held in sacred intention.

Co-regulation: The process by which one calm, regulated nervous system helps bring another dysregulated nervous system back into equilibrium. This is relational medicine. Your calm is the intervention.

Coercion: Any practice, however subtle or well-intentioned, that overrides a person's choice. In healing spaces, coercion often wears the language of encouragement. It is one of the fastest routes to nervous system activation for a trauma survivor.

Compassion Fatigue: The emotional, physical, and spiritual depletion that occurs when someone who holds space for others gives beyond their capacity without adequate replenishment. It is the cost of caring without protecting yourself.

Container: The felt sense of safety, predictability, and care that holds a space together. A container is both structural (agreements, logistics, environment) and relational (your presence, your regulation, the quality of your attention). Building the container is the foundation of all trauma-informed facilitation.

Content Disclaimer: A statement shared before introducing any material that might be activating. Disclaimers give people the information they need to make a sovereign choice about their participation. They are the practice of informed consent in real time.

Dissociation: A nervous system response in which the person disconnects from the present moment, their body, or their surroundings.

It is the system's way of creating distance from what feels unbearable. It can look like absence behind the eyes, a flat or foggy quality, or a person who appears calm but is unreachable.

Dysregulation: The state of being outside one's window of tolerance. When the nervous system is dysregulated, the capacity for clear thinking, emotional processing, and relational presence is diminished. It is a temporary state, and it responds to co-regulation, grounding, and safety.

Emotional Literacy: The capacity to identify, name, and communicate emotional experience. Many people have been taught to push through feeling or perform wellness. Part of trauma-informed work is gently expanding the vocabulary someone has for what lives inside them.

Epigenetics: The science of how lived experience can alter gene expression and be passed between generations. It is the biological basis for what many cultures have always known: that trauma, and healing, can ripple through a lineage.

Fawn Response: A stress response in which the body attempts to create safety through appeasement. Fawning looks like excessive agreeableness, over-compliance, smiling through pain, telling you what you want to hear. It is the response most likely to go undetected in a facilitation space, and one of the most important to understand.

Felt Sense: The body's internal knowing. A quality of awareness that lives beneath conscious thought. When you sense that something has shifted in a room before anyone speaks, you are accessing felt sense. It is the foundation of somatic awareness and attuned practice.

Fight Response: A stress response in which the body mobilizes for conflict. In facilitation spaces, it rarely looks like physical aggression. It is more likely to show as challenge, pushback, defensiveness, or a sharp quality in the voice. Underneath the armour is often profound fear.

Flight Response: A stress response in which the body mobilizes for escape. It looks like distraction, avoidance, fidgeting, restlessness, or a constant redirection away from what is activating. The person in flight is moving, physically or mentally, away from what feels unsafe.

Freeze Response: A stress response in which the body shuts down mobilization entirely. It can look like stillness, compliance, blankness, or a pleasant mask that does not quite reach the eyes. Freeze is the oldest of the stress responses and the one most often mistaken for calm.

Gaslighting: The act of making someone question the validity of their own experience. In healing spaces, it rarely arrives with malice. It arrives wearing compassion: reframes offered too quickly, spiritual explanations that bypass pain, or language that implies the person's response is the problem.

Grounding: Any practice that returns a person to present-moment awareness through the body and senses. Grounding is the antidote to activation. It anchors a person in the here and now so the nervous system can receive the signal that it is safe.

H.E.A.L. I.T.: A framework developed by Auroara Leigh for creating healing cultures. Humility. Equity. Antiracism. Lateral Kindness. Inclusivity. Trauma-Informed. It is a living orientation, a way of being in the world and in relationship.

Healership: The convergence of healing and leadership. Being a healed human who leads from that place. Healership recognises that the practitioner's own inner work is the foundation of everything they offer to others.

Informed Choice: The practice of giving people enough information to make a sovereign decision about their participation. It applies to content, activities, physical touch, emotional disclosure, and every moment where vulnerability is invited.

Integration: The process by which an experience becomes part of a person's understanding and embodiment. Without integration, powerful experiences, whether in ceremony, therapy, or facilitation, can leave doors open that a person is not resourced enough to walk through alone.

Intergenerational Trauma: Trauma that is transmitted across generations through biology, behaviour, narrative, and relational patterns. The grief that surfaces in a workshop circle may have roots that predate the person sitting in front of you. Generational healing is the intentional reversal of this pattern.

Interactional Synchrony: The subtle, often unconscious mirroring of rhythm, pace, and movement that occurs between two people in attuned relationship. It is one of the mechanisms by which co-regulation happens.

Lateral Kindness: Care that flows between equals rather than down from authority. In healing spaces, lateral kindness means treating every person as a sovereign, capable human deserving of dignity. It is one of the six pillars of the H.E.A.L. I.T. framework.

Mammalian Dive Reflex: A physiological response activated by cold water on the face, wrists, or neck. It produces a rapid shift in nervous system state by slowing the heart rate and redirecting blood flow. A simple, effective sensory reset tool.

P.A.C.E.: A four-step protocol for when you are triggered mid-session. Pause (take one breath). Acknowledge (name it to yourself silently). Contain (set your own material to the side with intention). Engage (return your full attention to the person).

Parasympathetic Nervous System: The branch of the autonomic nervous system responsible for rest, digestion, and recovery. When activated, it calms the body and supports the capacity for connection, clear thinking, and emotional processing. The longer exhale activates it.

Pathologizing: Treating a normal human response as a disorder or deficiency. In practice, it sounds like turning someone's grief into a diagnosis or framing their survival responses as symptoms to be managed. Trauma-informed practice refuses this lens.

Physiological Sigh: A breathing pattern identified by Stanford research as the fastest voluntary method for reducing stress: a double inhale through the nose followed by a long exhale through the mouth. It takes five seconds and is always available.

Polyvagal Theory: A theory developed by Stephen Porges describing how the vagus nerve mediates three distinct states of the nervous system: social engagement (safe), mobilisation (fight or flight), and immobilisation (freeze or shutdown). It provides the neurobiological foundation for understanding why safety is the precondition for healing.

Repair: The practice of acknowledging what happened when trust was strained, naming it with honesty, and tending to it with care. For many people, rupture without repair is the pattern they know. Offering repair is itself a healing act.

Rupture: A break in relational trust or safety within a facilitated space. Rupture is inevitable in any real relationship. What matters is whether it is followed by repair.

Sacred Witness: The posture at the heart of this book. To be present enough to hold what is, wise enough to sense what is being carried beneath it, and humble enough to let the person lead their own unfolding. Witnessing is medicine. It always has been.

Safer Space: The term used in place of "safe space" to acknowledge that no space can guarantee absolute safety. What we can do is commit to building a space that is as safe as it can possibly be, and to showing up with integrity when it falls short.

Self-Regulation: The ability to manage your own nervous system state. For a practitioner, self-regulation is your primary skill. Your regulated presence is the most powerful intervention available to you before any technique, before any framework, before any words.

Somatic: Of or relating to the body. In this book, somatic awareness refers to the practice of attending to sensation, breath, movement, and the felt experience of being in a body. The body holds what the mind may not yet have words for.

Sympathetic Nervous System: The branch of the autonomic nervous system responsible for mobilisation: the fight-or-flight response. When activated, it increases heart rate, sharpens focus, and prepares the body for action. It is the system that is running when someone is activated in your space.

Titration: The practice of carefully managing the intensity of emotional experience in a group or session. When one person's process is consuming the room's capacity, the practitioner gently creates a separate container for that process so the group can continue to be held.

Tracking: The somatic practice of following what is alive in another person's body and experience in real time. It is attending to words, tone, breath, movement, and the quality of presence simultaneously. Tracking feels like listening with the whole body.

Traum-our: Auroara Leigh's term for trauma-armour: the protective structures we build from unprocessed pain. Traum-our is the body's way of keeping us safe when safety was not available. It served its purpose. The work is learning when it is ready to come down.

Tuckman Model: Bruce Tuckman's four stages of group development: forming (orientation and politeness), storming (conflict and pushback), norming (finding rhythm and trust), and performing (deep, authentic work). In trauma-informed group facilitation, these stages cycle and repeat.

Vicarious Trauma: The cumulative psychological, emotional, and physiological impact of being repeatedly exposed to others' traumatic material. It is the cost of witnessing pain over time. It is real, it changes you at a cellular level, and it requires ongoing attention and care.

Window of Tolerance: The zone of nervous system arousal in which a person can function effectively: thinking clearly, feeling emotions without being overwhelmed, and maintaining relational connection. Above the window is hyperarousal (fight, flight). Below it is hypoarousal (freeze, shutdown). Knowing your own window is foundational to this work.

Ambiguous Loss: A form of grief for a loss that has no clear confirmation or resolution. Pauline Boss named the category. It includes the missing person, the alienated family member, the loved one with dementia who is physically present and psychically gone.

Co-regulation: The process by which one calm, regulated nervous system helps bring another dysregulated nervous system back toward safety. The oldest medicine the mammalian body knows.

Coercive Control: A pattern of domination through fear, isolation, surveillance, financial control, and emotional manipulation. It may or may not include physical violence. Named as a form of abuse by Evan Stark.

Disenfranchised Grief: Grief the surrounding culture does not offer rituals for. The loss of a pet. A miscarriage. An estranged relationship that is still alive. Still-valid grief without a public shape.

Glimmer: A micro-moment of safety the nervous system catches and registers. Deb Dana named them. Glimmers are the raw material of healing because they retrain the body to expect safety.

Minority Stress: The chronic, cumulative nervous system load that results from living in a society that treats your existence as contested. Documented particularly in LGBTQ2S+ and racialized populations.

Neuroception: Stephen Porges's term for the body's constant, unconscious scanning for cues of safety or danger. Neuroception decides how a body responds before the thinking mind catches up.

Polyvagal Ladder: Deb Dana's teaching image for the nervous system's three states: ventral vagal (safety and social engagement), sympathetic activation (fight and flight), and dorsal vagal shutdown (freeze and collapse).

Racialized Trauma: The specific somatic trauma pattern that results from living under chronic racialization. Described most clearly by Resmaa Menakem. Includes the body-level cost of microaggressions, macroaggressions, and inherited generational harm.

Self-Compassion: Kristin Neff's three-part practice: mindfulness of suffering, common humanity, and self-kindness. The direct antidote to shame.

Shame: The affect of believing the self is unworthy of belonging. Distinct from guilt, which is about an act. Shame is almost always distorted in trauma contexts and requires specific witnessing.

Sextortion: A form of digital abuse in which intimate images are obtained and used as leverage for money, more images, or control. A rising pattern particularly targeting teen boys.

Somatic Abolitionism: Resmaa Menakem's framework for the embodied, collective work of dismantling racialized harm through nervous system practice.

Soul Wound: Eduardo Duran's Indigenous-centred framework for intergenerational and historical trauma as a wound at the level of soul, not only psyche.

Vicarious Trauma: The emotional, physical, and spiritual impact on a helper of repeatedly witnessing trauma. Also called secondary traumatic stress or compassion fatigue. A predictable cost of sustained witnessing without aftercare.

Window of Tolerance: Daniel Siegel's term for the zone in which a person can feel, think, and engage without being overwhelmed. Above the window is hyperarousal; below is hypoarousal. Trauma narrows the window.

REFERENCES

Briere, J., & Scott, C. (2015). Principles of trauma therapy: A guide to symptoms, evaluation, and treatment (2nd ed.). Sage Publications.

Brown, R. P., & Gerbarg, P. L. (2005). Sudarshan Kriya yogic breathing in the treatment of stress, anxiety, and depression: Part I. Journal of Alternative and Complementary Medicine, 11(1), 189-201.

Figley, C. R. (Ed.). (1995). Compassion fatigue: Coping with secondary traumatic stress disorder in those who treat the traumatized. Brunner/Mazel.

Figley, C. R. (2002). Compassion fatigue: Psychotherapists' chronic lack of self-care. Journal of Clinical Psychology, 58(11), 1433-1441.

Fisher, J. (2017). Healing the fragmented selves of trauma survivors: Overcoming internal self-alienation. Routledge.

Kabat-Zinn, J. (2003). Mindfulness-based interventions in context: Past, present, and future. Clinical Psychology: Science and Practice, 10(2), 144-156.

Levine, P. A. (1997). Waking the tiger: Healing trauma. North Atlantic Books.

Levine, P. A. (2010). In an unspoken voice: How the body releases trauma and restores goodness. North Atlantic Books.

McCann, I. L., & Pearlman, L. A. (1990). Vicarious traumatization: A framework for understanding the psychological effects of working with victims. Journal of Traumatic Stress, 3(1), 131-149.

Neff, K. D. (2003). Self-compassion: An alternative conceptualization of a healthy attitude toward oneself. Self and Identity, 2(2), 85-101.

Ogden, P., Minton, K., & Pain, C. (2006). Trauma and the body: A sensorimotor approach to psychotherapy. W. W. Norton & Company.

Pearlman, L. A., & Saakvitne, K. W. (1995). Trauma and the therapist: Countertransference and vicarious traumatization in psychotherapy with incest survivors. W. W. Norton & Company.

Porges, S. W. (2011). The polyvagal theory: Neurophysiological foundations of emotions, attachment, communication, and self-regulation. W. W. Norton & Company.

Rothschild, B. (2006). Help for the helper: Self-care strategies for managing burnout and stress. W. W. Norton & Company.

Siegel, D. J. (1999). The developing mind: How relationships and the brain interact to shape who we are. Guilford Press.

Stamm, B. H. (2010). The concise ProQOL manual (2nd ed.). ProQOL.org.

Felitti, V. J., Anda, R. F., Nordenberg, D., Williamson, D. F., Spitz, A. M., Edwards, V., Koss, M. P., & Marks, J. S. (1998). Relationship of childhood abuse and household dysfunction to many of the leading causes of death in adults: The Adverse Childhood Experiences (ACE) Study. *American Journal of Preventive Medicine, 14*(4), 245-258.

World Health Organization. (2024). Violence against children. https://www.who.int/news-room/fact-sheets/detail/violence-against-children

van der Kolk, B. A. (2014). The body keeps the score: Brain, mind, and body in the healing of trauma. Viking.

If You or Someone You Know Needs Support

Healing takes courage. Sometimes the bravest thing a person can do is reach out.

Crisis and Suicide Prevention International Association for Suicide Prevention directory: https://www.iasp.info/resources/Crisis_Centres/ 988 Suicide and Crisis Lifeline (US): Call or text 988 Crisis Services Canada: 1-833-456-4566 or text 45645 Samaritans (UK): 116 123 Befrienders Worldwide (30+ countries): https://befrienders.org

Mental Health and Trauma Support Crisis Text Line: Text HOME to 741741 (US), 686868 (Canada), 85258 (UK), or 50808 (Ireland) Open Counseling international therapist directory: https://www.opencounseling.com

Domestic Violence National Domestic Violence Hotline (US): 1-800-799-7233 or text START to 88788 Shelter Safe (Canada): https://sheltersafe.ca

Indigenous-Specific Support Hope for Wellness Help Line (First Nations, Inuit, Métis): 1-855-242-3310 Indian Residential Schools Crisis Line: 1-866-925-4419

Finding a Trauma-Informed Practitioner Psychology Today therapist directory: https://www.psychologytoday.com EMDR International Association: https://www.emdria.org Somatic Experiencing International: https://directory.traumahealing.org

More Free Resources: https://simplysacred.ca/the-healing-journey

You do not have to carry this alone. Reaching out is one of the most sacred acts of self-care a human being can choose.

Expanded Reading for This Edition

Boss, P. (1999). Ambiguous Loss: Learning to Live with Unresolved Grief. Harvard University Press.

Brown, B. (2012). Daring Greatly: How the Courage to Be Vulnerable Transforms the Way We Live, Love, Parent, and Lead. Gotham Books.

Buqué, M. (2024). Break the Cycle: A Guide to Healing Intergenerational Trauma. Dutton.

Dana, D. (2018). The Polyvagal Theory in Therapy: Engaging the Rhythm of Regulation. W. W. Norton.

Delahooke, M. (2022). Brain-Body Parenting: How to Stop Managing Behavior and Start Raising Joyful, Resilient Kids. Harper Wave.

Devine, M. (2017). It's OK That You're Not OK: Meeting Grief and Loss in a Culture That Doesn't Understand. Sounds True.

Duran, E. (2006). Healing the Soul Wound: Counseling with American Indians and Other Native Peoples. Teachers College Press.

Hemphill, P. (2024). What It Takes to Heal: How Transforming Ourselves Can Change the World. Random House.

Herman, J. (2015). Trauma and Recovery: The Aftermath of Violence. Basic Books.

Linklater, R. (2014). Decolonizing Trauma Work: Indigenous Stories and Strategies. Fernwood Publishing.

Maté, G. (2003). When the Body Says No: Exploring the Stress-Disease Connection. Wiley.

Maté, G. (2022). The Myth of Normal: Trauma, Illness, and Healing in a Toxic Culture. Avery.

Menakem, R. (2017). My Grandmother's Hands: Racialized Trauma and the Pathway to Mending Our Hearts and Bodies. Central Recovery Press.

Methot, S. (2019). Legacy: Trauma, Story, and Indigenous Healing. ECW Press.

Mullan, J. (2023). Decolonizing Therapy: Oppression, Historical Trauma, and Politicizing Your Practice. W. W. Norton.

Neff, K. (2011). Self-Compassion: The Proven Power of Being Kind to Yourself. William Morrow.

Perry, B., & Winfrey, O. (2021). What Happened to You? Conversations on Trauma, Resilience, and Healing. Flatiron Books.

Piepzna-Samarasinha, L. L. (2018). Care Work: Dreaming Disability Justice. Arsenal Pulp Press.

Price, D. (2022). Unmasking Autism: Discovering the New Faces of Neurodiversity. Harmony.

Real, T. (1997). I Don't Want to Talk About It: Overcoming the Secret Legacy of Male Depression. Scribner.

Schwartz, R. (2021). No Bad Parts: Healing Trauma and Restoring Wholeness with the Internal Family Systems Model. Sounds True.

Siegel, D. J., & Bryson, T. P. (2011). The Whole-Brain Child. Delacorte Press.

Stark, E. (2007). Coercive Control: How Men Entrap Women in Personal Life. Oxford University Press.

Vaid-Menon, A. (2020). Beyond the Gender Binary. Penguin Workshop.

van Dernoot Lipsky, L. (2009). Trauma Stewardship: An Everyday Guide to Caring for Self While Caring for Others. Berrett-Koehler.

Walker, P. (2013). Complex PTSD: From Surviving to Thriving. Azure Coyote.

Walker, R. (2020). The Unapologetic Guide to Black Mental Health. New Harbinger.

Weller, F. (2015). The Wild Edge of Sorrow: Rituals of Renewal and the Sacred Work of Grief. North Atlantic Books.

www.ingramcontent.com/pod-product-compliance
Lightning Source LLC
LaVergne TN
LVHW050817061126
851857LV00012B/847